ELEMENTARY SCHOOL LIBRARIAN'S SURVIVAL GUIDE

Ready-to-use tips, techniques,
and materials to help you save time
and work in virtually every aspect
of your job

Barbara Farley Bannister • Janice B. Carlile

ILLUSTRATIONS BY KATHY BARON

THE CENTER FOR APPLIED
RESEARCH IN EDUCATION
West Nyack, New York 10995

© 1993 by

THE CENTER FOR APPLIED
RESEARCH IN EDUCATION
West Nyack, New York

10 9 8 7 6 5 4 3 2 1

Library of Congress Cataloging-in-Publication Data

Bannister, Barbara Farley.
    The elementary school librarian's survival guide / Barbara Farley
Banister, Janice B. Carlile ; illustrations by Kathy Baron.
      p. cm.
    ISBN 0-87628-297-4
     1. School libraries--United States--Administration.   I. Carlile,
Janice B. II. Title

Z675.S3B234 1993   93-17556
027.8'222'0973--dc20   CIP

ISBN 0-87628-297-4

**The Center for Applied Research
in Education,** Professional Publishing
West Nyack, New York 10995

Simon & Schuster, A Paramount Communications Company

Printed in the United States of America

DEDICATION

To the students and staff of Memorial School for making the LMC activities a joy!

Barbara Bannister

To the students and staff at Adams School, who provided me with many opportunities to grow as a librarian, and to my husband, who prepared many wonderful meals as this book was being written.

Jan Carlile

ACKNOWLEDGMENTS

Thanks to Patty Waltz and Betsy Wheeler for the ideas for Authors' Day.

ABOUT THE AUTHORS

Barbara Bannister has been the media specialist/librarian at Memorial Elementary School for twenty years. She has also taught language arts enrichment and kindergarten, 2nd, 3rd, and 5th grades.

Mrs. Bannister graduated from Western Michigan University in Kalamazoo, Michigan and has taken graduate work from Portland State University and Western Oregon State. She is the author of several books including *Media Center Activities For Every Month of the School Year*, *Reading Roundups*, *Reading Bingos, Puzzles, and Research Activities for the Elementary School Year*, and *The New Elementary School Librarian's Almanac*.

Janice Carlile has been an elementary school media specialist/librarian at Adams School in McMinnville for fifteen years.

Mrs. Carlile earned her B. A. from Linfield College in McMinnville and did graduated work at Portland State University and Western Oregon State College.

ABOUT THIS BOOK

The Elementary School Librarian's Survival Guide is designed to help the busy librarian and media specialist successfully handle the many situations they encounter throughout the school year—the budget crunch, the flood of new materials, constantly changing technology, and maintaining student disciplines. It includes numerous time-saving forms, notes, activities, and schedules that can be copied for immediate use. Much of the attractive artwork throughout the guide can also be used for other purposes, such as bulletin boards and bookmarks.

For easy use, the guide is divided into eleven convenient sections that focus on a particular area of your LMC (library and media center). Here's a sampling of what you can expect to find in each of the sections:

The Physical Organization and Management of Your LMC — Tips on how to arrange the various sections of your LMC for the most efficient operation of your programs; materials and ideas for making your LMC attractive and inviting; the advantages and disadvantages of flexible and fixed scheduling.

Successful Discipline — Effective room plans and challenging programs that help control disruptive behavior; tested techniques and strategies for working with the school staff to promote successful discipline; a useful guide to help a substitute discipline handle problems in your LMC.

Reading Promotions — Brief descriptions of commercial reading programs to help you select those appropriate for your library; three original reading promotions for use in your LMC; ways to promote books and reading with effective advertising.

Running Special Programs — Ideas for displays and author and speaker visits; various activities to make your LMC an exciting, fun-filled place.

Storytimes, Book Talks, and Library Skills — How to make storytimes and book talks more intriguing; activities that make library skills more interesting for students; ready-to-use patterns for many storytime themes.

Building Support With the Administration, Faculty, Parents and Community — Numerous forms and letters to promote and build support for your LMC; suggestions enable you to be an available and willing resource; ways to promote rapport with staff, administration, and parents.

Budgeting for Success — Ways to evaluate your present budget and plan for suggestions for future budgets; carefully using your funds; additional ways to fund your LMC activities.

Selection Policies, Censorship, and Copyright — How to deal with challenges to your selections; what to do about censorship and copyright; helpful guidelines on copyrighted materials.

Keeping Up With New Materials and Surviving Technology — How to keep up with the flood of new materials and technology; a specific needs checklist if you plan to computerize; ordering information for periodicals.

Inventory and Weeding — Forms that help you know what has been weeded and what needs replacement; how to justify time for inventory and weeding through an effective letter presented to administrators.

Avoiding Burnout: Enjoying Your Job to the Fullest! — How to keep your enthusiasm for work in the LMC: a detailed job description to foster staff and administration understanding of your work; establish good rapport with students.

The Elementary Librarian's Survival Guide puts at your fingertips many ideas and ready-to-use materials for the efficient management of your LMC. We hope you will use and enjoy the book for many years to come.

Barbara Bannister and Jan Carlile

CONTENTS

About This Book

Chapter One   THE PHYSICAL ORGANIZATION
AND MANAGEMENT OF YOUR LMC 1

ROOM ORGANIZATION 3

   Checkout and Book Return Area 3

   Card Catalog 4

   Fiction Section 4

   Easy (Everybody) Section 4

   Nonfiction Section 5

   Reference Section 5

   Periodicals Section 6

   Storytelling Area 6

   Skills-Teaching Area 6

   Audiovisual Area 7

   Skill/Think Games Area 7

   Librarian's Work Area 7

   Storage Area 7

   More Ideas for a Workable and Attractive LMC 8

TIME MANAGEMENT 9

   Planning Your Class Schedules 9

      Flexible Scheduling. 9

         Reproducibles:

            May We Come? 10

            Keeping Track. 11

      Fixed Scheduling 12

   Planning for LMC Management 13

      Reproducible:

         Student Library Assistant Application 14

CIRCULATION MANAGEMENT 15

   Checkout 15

Returning Materials to the LMC 16

How to Recover Books 17

Reproducibles:

Note for Reserving Books 18

Sample Banner 19

Sample Overdue Notes 19

Student Withdrawal From School Form 20

Sample Letter Sent to Another School After a Student Withdraws 21

Sample Letter to Parents for Overdue Books 22

Sample Letter to Parents for Damaged Books 23

Sample Poster for End-of-the-Year Book Returns 24

Chapter Two   SUCCESSFUL DISCIPLINE 25

ROOM ARRANGEMENT 27

A CHALLENGING PROGRAM 27

A WORKABLE PLAN FOR LMC CONDUCT 29

Reproducibles:

Notes for Classroom Teacher 30

Good Job Chart 31

WORKING WITH STAFF ON YOUR DISCIPLINE PLAN 32

A DISCIPLINE PLAN FOR YOUR SUBSTITUTE 33

Reproducible:

Schedule and Discipline Plan for Your Substitute 34

Chapter Three   READING PROMOTIONS 35

READING PROMOTIONS 37

Commercial Reading Programs 37

Your Own Reading Programs 38

"My State" Reading Promotion 38

Reproducibles:

Parent Note 40

Bookmarks 40

My State Reading Club Certificate 41

Bicycle Patterns for Recording Students' Progress 42

Student Record Sheet for My State Reading Club 43

"Johnny Appleseed" Reading Promotion 44

Reproducibles:

Parent Letter 45

Bulletin Board Patterns for the Johnny Appleseed Readers Club 46

Johnny Appleseed Reading Club Certificate 47

Apple Book Finders 48

Apple Scavenger Hunt 49

"Read Along the Rainbow Road" Reading Promotion 50

Reproducibles:

Bulletin Board Patterns 51

Parent Note & Record Sheet 52

Read Along the Rainbow Readers Club Certificate 53

Card Catalog Capers 54

Rainbow Shelf Search 55

ADVERTISING BOOKS AND READING 56

Reproducible:

Addresses for Commercial Reading Promotions 58

Chapter Four   RUNNING SPECIAL PROGRAMS 59

EXHIBITS AND DISPLAYS 61

Student Exhibits 61

Reproducible:

Sample Notes for Student Exhibits 62

Exhibits From Parents and Faculty 63

Reproducibles:

Exhibits Wanted 63

Thank You Note 63

SPEAKERS AND DEMONSTRATIONS 64

FOCUS ON FUN 66

Autumn Fun 66

Reproducibles:

Pumpkins 67

Cat Shapes 67

Pattern for Turkey Tale Creating Writing 68

Winter and Holiday Fun 69

Reproducibles:

Holiday "Guesstimation" 69

Patterns for Question Ornaments 72

Patterns for "Pick a Winner" Winter Activity 73

Spring Fun 74

Any-Time-of-Year Activities 75

Student Authors' Day 75

Reproducibles:

Book Comment Sheet 77

Autograph Signing Form 78

Sample Authors' Day Program 79

SUGGESTIONS FOR GROUP LEADERS 80

Reproducibles:

Group Leader Guidelines for Helping Students Share Books 81

Authors' Certificate 82

School Book of Academic Records 83

Reproducibles:

Sample Cover for School Book of Academic Records 85

Sample Form for Record Holder Pages 86

Chapter Five STORYTIMES, BOOK TALKS, AND LIBRARY SKILLS 87

STORYTIMES 89

Storytime Rules 89

Storytime Props 89

Student Involvement 90

Storytime Suggestions 91

Reproducibles:

Patterns for The Little Engine That Could and Inch by Inch 92

Patterns for "The Twelve Days of Halloween" Cards 93

BOOK TALKS 96

LIBRARY SKILLS 98

   Suggestions for Library Skills Plans 98

   Hands-On and Written Activities 99

   The Curriculum Connection 100

     Reproducibles:

       Let's Find It 101

       It Happened in January! 102

       Dictionary Daze for St. Patrick's Day 103

Chapter Six   **BUILDING SUPPORT WITH THE ADMINISTRATION,
FACULTY, AND COMMUNITY** 105

BUILDING SUPPORT WITH YOUR FACULTY 107

   Be an Available, Willing Resource 107

     Reproducibles:

       School Calendar 108

       Request Form for Materials 109

       Request Form for New Books and Audiovisual Materials 110

       Response Notes for Requests 111

   Be Fair 112

     Reproducibles:

       Form for Audiovisual Checklist 113

       Sample Headings for LMC Newsletters 114

       LMC Invitation to Browse 117

       Welcome to your LMC — Request Form 117

   Keep Your Faculty Informed 118

   Be An Active Participant 118

   Be Aware and Concerned 118

BUILDING SUPPORT WITH YOUR ADMINISTRATOR 119

   Keeping Your Administrator Informed 119

   Be Professional — Working With Your Administrator 120

BUILDING GOOD RELATIONSHIPS WITH PARENTS AND THE COMMUNITY 120

BUILDING GOOD RELATIONS WITH YOUR CUSTODIAN 120

Reproducible:

"Please Help" Form and Thank You Note 121

Keeping Them Informed 122

Reproducibles:

Dear Parents Letter 123

Helping Children Become Better Readers 124

Summer Is Here! A Perfect Time to Read! 125

Provide Useful Information 126

Solicit Their Involvement 126

Reproducibles:

Sample Volunteer Letter to Parents 128

Sample Volunteer Letter to Civic Groups 129

Chapter Seven BUDGETING FOR SUCCESS 131

TAKING STOCK OF YOUR PRESENT BUDGET
AND PLANNING WITH YOUR SUPERVISORS 133

Reproducible:

Proposed Budget Plan 134

OTHER SOURCES FOR FUNDING 135

Book Fairs 135

Parent-Teacher Organizations 136

Donations and Service Organizations 136

Used-Book Sale 136

Reproducible:

Sample Letter to Parents Explaining Why Books Are Being Sold 137

Grants 138

MAKING CAREFUL USE OF FUNDS 138

Reproducibles:

Sample Form for Your "Wish List" Card file 139

Budget Form 140

Chapter Eight   SELECTION POLICIES, CENSORSHIP, AND COPYRIGHT 141

SELECTION POLICIES 143

CENSORSHIP 144

    Reproducibles:

        Sample letter to Complainant 146

        Sample Citizen's Request Form for Revaluation of Materials 147

COPYRIGHT 149

    Quick Facts About Video Copyright 150

    Guidelines to Video Off-Air Recording 150

    Reproducibles:

        Copyright Notice Form 150

        Copyright Notice Sign 151

Chapter Nine   **KEEPING UP WITH NEW MATERIALS
AND SURVIVING TECHNOLOGY** 153

KEEPING UP WITH NEW MATERIALS 155

    Professional Journals 155

    Other Ways to Learn About New Materials 156

    Ordering Periodicals for Staff and Students 156

    Reproducibles:

        Periodical Survey Form for Staff 157

        Periodical Survey Form for Students 157

        Form for Requesting Materials 158

    Ordering Times 159

SURVIVING TECHNOLOGY 159

    Computerization of the LMC 160

      Advantages 160

      Disadvantages 160

    District Planning 161

    Reproducibles:

        Sample Letter and Sample Questionnaire
        to Library Computerization Companies 162

    Other Technology Concerns 166

    Reproducibles:

        Available Technology — Equipment 167

        Available Technology — Software 168

Chapter Ten   INVENTORY AND WEEDING 169

    HINTS FOR INVENTORY AND WEEDING 172

    WEEDING GUIDELINES 172

    WHAT TO DO WHEN INVENTORY IS COMPLETED 175

    MAKING PROVISIONS FOR WITHDRAWN BOOKS 175
       Reproducibles:
          Inventory and Weeding Charts 176

Chapter Eleven AVOIDING BURNOUT: Enjoying Your Job to the Fullest 191

    JOB DESCRIPTION FOR SECURITY 194

    GOOD RELATIONSHIPS WITH STAFF AND ADMINISTRATION 196

    GOOD RAPPORT WITH STUDENTS 197
       Reproducible:
          Let' Hear Your Ideas 197

    WELL-PLANNED PROGRAM OF LIBRARY ACTIVITIES 198

    DELEGATE TASKS TO ASSISTANTS AND VOLUNTEERS 199
       Reproducibles:
          Volunteer Survey 200
          LMC Responsibilities Chart 201

    ATTEND STIMULATING, INSPIRATIONAL WORKSHOPS AND SEMINARS 202

    VISIT OTHER SUCCESSFUL LIBRARY/MEDIA CENTERS 202
       Reproducibles:
          Permission Form for Workshops and Seminars 203
          Forms Requesting Permission to Visit Another LMC
          and for Inviting Media Specialists to Visit Your LMC 204

    TIME TO CONNECT WITH OTHER LIBRARIANS 204

    BOOK-SHOPPING TRIPS WITH OTHER LIBRARIANS 204

    SAVING TIME FOR YOURSELF AND YOUR FAMILY 206

THE LIBRARIAN'S REFRAIN

It's 7:30 a.m. and here I am,
Ready for another day.
I'll turn on the computer, file some cards,
And put some books away!

Here comes the fourth grade teacher,
I know just what she needs,
Some information on our state,
That's all she ever reads.

Now let's see . . . where was I?
Oh, yes, I'll file a card or two,
I'd like to get these filed today,
But there's so much else to do!

Oh, the doors are opening,
It's time for the kids to arrive,
I didn't get much done so far,
Oh, how will I survive?

"Can I check out this video?"
"Where is the vertical file?"
"It's MY turn on the computer,
You can just wait awhile!"

"My teacher needs a book on frogs,
My report is on a bear.
I looked for it in the card catalog,
But I couldn't find it there!"

"Check my book out—HURRY!
You know I can't be late!
My teacher will give me detention,
That's something I just hate!"

School is starting - they're leaving!
Maybe I can get something done,
I might even get the books shelved,
If I can do it on the run!

Oh, no, here's my first class,
Just eight more to go today.
I might as well forget those books,
They don't need shelving anyway!

Oh, here comes a boy with a goldfish,
And a girl with a bug in a jar,
They want to know all about them,
Well, the science section's not far.

Lunchtime at last and time for my break
But here comes Miss Jones for a book.
She needs it right now to read to her class,
And she doesn't have time to look!

Oh, well, I wasn't too hungry,
I ate breakfast five hours ago,
The kindergarten's ready for stories,
And I have puppets to show.

Storytimes, book talks, and reference,
And card catalog skills galore . . .
Oh, now what is that noise I hear?
The "C" drawer's dropped on the floor!

I have to teach atlases and almanacs,
Dictionaries and encyclopedias too!
How can I ever cover them all?
How will I ever get through?

The bulletin boards need changing . . .
How could this whole month be gone?
It's time to order books again,
I guess I should stay here 'til dawn!

I look at the clock and I shudder,
It just can't be the time to go!
I didn't even get those cards filed,
BUT I DID HELP YOUNG MINDS TO GROW!

Chapter One

THE PHYSICAL ORGANIZATION AND MANAGEMENT OF YOUR LMC

Whether you are an excited media specialist who just graduated from college or an experienced specialist in a library or media center, take the time to look objectively at your LMC. Organizing your LMC attractively and effectively is one of the most important things you can do to ensure a productive and happy year for you and the students.

ROOM ORGANIZATION

Some areas that need to be considered for their best placement to ensure effective use and good traffic flow are

- Check-out Station and Book Return
- Card Catalog (or computer stations for catalog search)
- Fiction Section
- Nonfiction Section
- Picture Book (sometimes called "Easy" or "Everybody") Section
- Reference Section
- Periodicals Section
- Area for Storytelling
- Area for Skills Classes
- Area for Use of Audiovisual Materials
- Area for Use of Skill and Think-Type Games
- Librarian's Work Area
- Storage Area

You are fortunate if you have a spacious facility that allows you to keep these sections relatively separate, but most facilities in schools are basically rectangular. The following are some suggestions for the location of needed areas in your LMC. Choose those that apply to your particular facility.

Checkout and Book Return Area

Often your checkout and book return area are built in, so you have little control over where this section can be located. However, if you are planning a new LMC or if your checkout desk and book return are moveable, try to plan for them to be located near an exit. This helps students remember to check out their materials as they go past this area when leaving. It also provides them with immediate access to the book return area when they enter the library. Most importantly, try to be sure that this area has a clear view of the entire LMC, because you will be spending a great deal of time here — either checking out books or checking them in. A large attractive sign posted to proclaim the checkout area, and another sign placed over the book return area may help students remember to return their books. These signs may be purchased from library supply stores or you can make them yourselves.

Whether your station is computerized or a manual checkout, make certain there is enough counter space for you to check books in and out. Keep in mind that students need room to put down their books while checking out. In a noncomputerized situation, you could have a small table nearby for students to sign their book cards before bringing them to the checkout counter. If at all possible, reserve room behind the book return area for a cart on which you can place the checked-in books.

Card Catalog

The card catalog must be centrally located but not in a traffic pattern. If you are using computerized stations for catalog search, you will probably have three to four stations placed in different areas of your LMC to avoid congestion. Avoid placing these stations at the storytelling or picture book section.

Fiction Section

Shelves should be a reasonable height for browsing. If you have built-in shelves and the top shelf is too high for most students, save these shelves for displaying new books or book character dolls. Letter labels on the shelves or on signs above the shelves facilitate student ease in finding books. An overstuffed chair or a sofa is a warm addition to any library and encourages students to browse or read.

Some librarians place spine labels on books to identify genre — such as animal fiction, science fiction, mystery, and so on. Others prefer to let children discover the genre on their own. Such labels may be purchased from library supply companies.

A helpful addition to the fiction section is a small free-standing bookcase where new books or Newbery books can be featured. A sign above or on top of this bookcase could proclaim the area as the "Newbery Nest" and the other side of the case as "Notable New Books."

Make your fiction section as comfortable and attractive as possible. This may be the place where students discover the joy of reading.

Easy (Everybody) Section

Low shelves (approximately 40 to 50 inches high) are essential for this section so that young students can reach the books. The shelves need to be at least 13 to 14 inches apart to accommodate the oversized books common to this collection.

Letter-labeling the shelves will help young students who are just learning to locate books. If possible, leave room on the top of the bookcases for stuffed storybook characters or other displays. Low tables and chairs or bright-colored cushions are conducive to easy browsing and comfortable reading. A small rocking chair or two are happy additions to this section.

Nonfiction Section

When possible, this section should be located near both the reference section and the card catalog or computer search stations for efficient research.

Each section of this area can be labeled with attractive posters showing the Dewey Decimal number. These signs can be purchased from library supply houses or you can make your own.

A table or two with several chairs should be placed in this section so that students have an area in which to work on their research.

Make sure there is enough room to display such things as dinosaur models, rocks, and craft examples, in order to advertise the many books located here. If you do not have a display case or room for one, the tops of the bookcases or the top shelves may be reserved for displays. A bulletin board for advertising nonfiction books or for research-type questions adds interest.

Reference Section

Locate this section near the nonfiction section in a quiet area away from excess traffic. Shelves should be fairly far apart to accommodate various-sized reference sources, such as atlases. A sign advertising the area as the "Reference" section will prove helpful and will be attractive. There needs to be at least one table with several chairs in or near this section for students to spend time on research projects.

Included in this section should be the following resources: encyclopedias, almanacs, dictionaries, thesaurus, biographical dictionaries, geographical dictionaries, books of quotations, *Guinness Book of World Records*, a sample of the

Reader's Guide or a children's magazine guide, and children's author biographical sources such as the *Junior Book of Authors*. An area for newspapers could be in this section also.

Periodicals Section

Built-in shelves for periodicals are a great addition to your facility, although most LMCs will not have them. A portable magazine rack should probably be placed in the fiction section since this is where most browsing will occur. If you have space, it would be good to put periodicals for younger children, such as *Humpty Dumpty*, *Scienceland*, and *Ranger Rick* in the picture book section of the library. When you have only one rack for periodicals, magazines for younger children could just be placed on the tables in the picture book section.

Labels on the magazine rack designating each magazine are helpful. Many LMCs provide plastic covers for the new magazines, which can be purchased at library supply houses. Ask student helpers to help you complete this time-consuming task. These plastic covers denote new magazines and those that may not be checked out

Storytelling Area

The ideal location for this section is in the picture book/easy section. Regardless of the location, however, it should be comfortable for both the storyteller and the children. The area should not be near a door or other trafficked areas to avoid distractions during storytime. Some LMCs have a built-in story well or stage steps where the children can sit. A low chair for the storyteller needs to be in front of the area where the children sit. If steps are not available, soft, bright-colored cushions may be placed for the students to sit on. However, avoid supplying pillows unless you have enough for all the children, since they will be tempted to run for them. You may wish to have a cupboard or a table near the storytelling chair to hold books or props that you plan to use during the storytelling.

Skills-Teaching Area

This area needs enough tables with chairs to accommodate your largest class (ideally, sixteen or fewer!). A chalkboard or dry-erase board should be part of this area. A bulletin board where you can post skills game boards is also helpful. To use this area effectively, try to keep it out of a traffic pattern.

Audiovisual Area

Locate the area for audiovisual use as near your work area as possible because you may be called upon to assist with the various pieces of equipment. Some pieces of equipment that you might consider providing in this area are sound-filmstrip machines, cassette tape players, record players, TV/VCR, and computers. The software to be used by individual children for these various pieces of equipment can be stored near or in this area to ease traffic and confusion. Audiovisual software for classroom use should probably be stored elsewhere.

Skill/Think Games Area

The games for this area should be checked out for LMC use from the checkout desk to ensure that they are properly returned. If you don't have space for a game area, the games can be placed on tables in the fiction or picture book section. You may prefer not to have these available in your LMC unless you feel that they are a good addition to your facility. Games you might consider for this area are strategy games, such as chess, checkers, Battleship, Stratego, Moncala (African Rock Game), and Mastermind.

Librarian's Work Area

This area should be ample in size for book repair, cataloging, bulletin board preparation, lesson planning, and so forth. Be sure there is adequate counter space with cupboards or shelves above. Ideally, this area should be enclosed, with a large window area for viewing the rest of the LMC.

Storage Area

You are fortunate if you have space for audiovisual software, equipment, and display items. When space is tight and you do not have a room for these things, try to assign all of the equipment to the various classrooms. Store the software either in your work area or filed with the books on your shelves. When stored in the work area, all of the software is quickly obtainable. However, when filed with the books, the pertinent software is adjacent to them and can be easily located.

Try to have the storage area well-lighted. Store small items such as batteries or replacement bulbs for equipment in labeled containers that are then filed on shelves in alphabetical order. Organize the software by Dewey Decimal number so that you can find it quickly. You may prefer to check out the equipment as needed, but be sure to organize a traffic pattern and label shelves for each piece of equipment stored there.

Display items can be stored on shelves, with labels for the items such as Horse Collection Display or Dinosaur Models. Seasonal displays can be shelved together and labeled Halloween, Thanksgiving, Christmas, and so on.

In short, proper organization of your storage area saves valuable time when gathering material for your use or for the use of the teachers.

More Ideas for a Workable and Attractive LMC

The well-organized and well-planned placement of various areas in your LMC is, of course, the most effective way to a workable, attractive facility. There are, however, little extras that you can do to make your LMC a welcoming place for students.

A lovely "extra" is a tropical fish tank placed in any of the browsing sections, such as the fiction, nonfiction, or easy section. The fish are a colorful and interesting attraction, adding a beautiful touch to your LMC. Place books about tropical fish near the aquarium so that students can read about them. Maintenance of a fish tank is work, of course, but you will find that once the tank is established, there is not much to do other than feeding the fish. Your student assistants will be happy to care for both the fish and the tank for you.

Another attractive addition that will also make your facility more exciting and interesting is a bird cage, especially a large one. Consider keeping birds like parakeets, some finches, canaries, myna birds, or a parrot. These pets require more work than a fish tank, but, again, you will find many student aides willing to care for them.

Fresh flowers on the checkout desk and a few potted plants in windows or other well-lighted spots add beauty and warmth to your surroundings.

TIME MANAGEMENT

Planning Your Class Schedules

You may choose to schedule your classes according to either a fixed or a flexible schedule. You and your staff will have to determine which is best for your particular school. There are both benefits and disadvantages to each type.

Flexible Scheduling

Basically, flexible scheduling is a looser arrangement of class times. Large blocks of time are left open so that teachers may schedule periods of research, literature appreciation, or needed skill instruction. With this type of scheduling you will need to work closely with each teacher to assure that all classes are being served for both recreational reading and research skills.

You may wish to combine flexible and rigid scheduling. For example, you may wish to have kindergarten, grade one, and grade two students scheduled for a regular weekly slot for storytimes and checkout. The other grades can then schedule their own times when needed in the remaining time slots. A form (May We Come?) for scheduling requests is included here. The requests for skills time in the LMC should be scheduled in connection with work being taught in the classroom. For example, a class learning about the American Revolution might schedule time in the LMC to work with the card catalog in order to find books on this subject, or to work with encyclopedias. Another class studying their state might schedule time in the LMC to have the media specialist teach them the use of the almanac to find out their state's nickname, products, and population.

As the media specialist, you need to be aware of what skills have been taught to each grade. It is a little more difficult with flexible scheduling — you will find that some teachers are diligent in scheduling times for instruction related to their class work, while other teachers have to be sought out to be sure their classes have received the necessary skills. A form (Keeping Track) is provided in this chapter for your records.

With flexible scheduling, you can develop a closer working relationship with teachers, provide for a more meaningful teaching of skills, and allow more time for special programs. However, it is harder to ensure that each student is provided with opportunities for both recreational reading and for research skills. Sometimes it may be difficult to think of something in the curriculum that stimulates learning how to use some reference books. You may find it even more difficult to work with each teacher to be sure that his/her class has received the necessary skills instruction.

MAY WE COME?

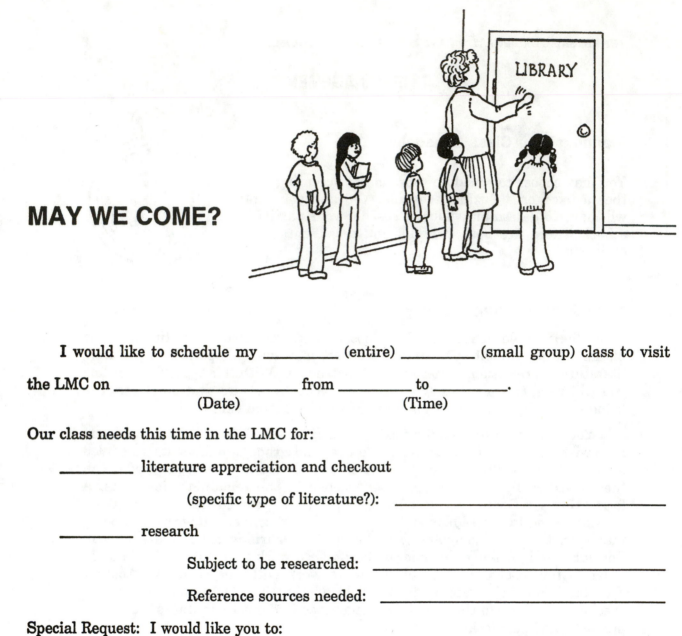

I would like to schedule my _____ (entire) _____ (small group) class to visit

the LMC on _____ from _____ to _____.
                          (Date)   (Time)

Our class needs this time in the LMC for:

_____ literature appreciation and checkout

           (specific type of literature?): _____

_____ research

           Subject to be researched: _____

           Reference sources needed: _____

Special Request: I would like you to:

_____
                        (Teacher)

KEEPING TRACK

Skills Taught by Grade. Enter date taught in proper space.

SKILL	GRADE 3	GRADE 4	GRADE 5	GRADE 6
Parts of a Book				
Fact/Fiction Books				
Dewey Decimal System				
Locating Books				
Card Catalog Use				
Almanacs				
Atlas				
Dictionary				
Encyclopedia				
Biographical Dictionary				
Geographical Dictionary				
Thesaurus				
Book of Quotations				
Junior Book of Authors				
Reader's Guide				
Vertical File				
AV Instruction				

LITERATURE APPRECIATION	GRADE 3	GRADE 4	GRADE 5	GRADE 6
Modern Fiction				
Historical Fiction				
Science Fiction and Fantasy				
Mystery and Adventure				
Biography and Autobiography				
Nonfiction				

Fixed Scheduling

In fixed scheduling, each classroom is scheduled into the LMC at a regular time each week. In grades where formal skills are taught, the classes should be scheduled half a class at a time for more effective instruction.

At the beginning of the year, the teacher and the media specialist need to schedule the weekly time slots for the year. The media specialist should promote and encourage the scheduling of classes at a time when students are receptive to books and reading. For example, an LMC time slot after P.E. or recess should be avoided if possible because students may be too excited or exhausted to listen well.

There are many advantages to fixed scheduling:

- The students are aware of when they will be coming to the LMC so they will be ready to return books at that time.

- All students will be sure of spending time in the LMC each week.

- The LMC specialist will be able to keep track of skills taught to each class.

Whichever type of scheduling is decided upon for your school, try not to let class time in the LMC be used as a prep time for teachers. You are teaching the students valuable learning tools that they will use for life; therefore, their time with you should be scheduled in their best interests. For example, teaching specific skills to an entire class when working with smaller groups would be more effective is not good for the students and should not be acceptable if the purpose is just to give the classroom teacher more planning time.

Planning for LMC Management

As a media specialist, you are aware of the many tasks that must be done in order to have an effective, well-organized media program. If you allow yourself to become too fully scheduled with classes, you will not have time for adequate library management. Although these management tasks may vary from one LMC to another, there are some that are common to all media centers. Some of these are budgeting, ordering materials, cataloging, circulation of materials, card catalog maintenance, mending of books, weeding, shelving, preparing bibliographies, keeping abreast of new materials through reviews in professional publications, filling teacher requests, arranging special programs (such as author visits), preparing overdue lists, sending notices home to parents, and planning for library programs as well as for individual class sessions.

Obviously, these tasks cannot be accomplished during before or after school hours, so be sure to block in some time each day for these responsibilities. Try to arrange your schedule so that your library management blocks of time are at least an hour long. These hours will undoubtedly be often interrupted, but at least you can hope to get some of these tasks accomplished.

When you find yourself with a short period of free time now and then, there are some things that can be done in 10 or 15 minutes, such as shelving a few books, reading shelves, or checking in some books. Don't try to mend books, prepare bibliographies, enter book titles in your computer, or any task that requires time or uninterrupted concentration.

These tasks appear insurmountable but volunteers or paid aides can make them less overwhelming. If you are lucky enough to have a paid assistant, he/she can do many of the tasks that must be completed. Some jobs that may be relegated to your assistant could be shelving, the filing of catalog cards (or posting the book titles to your computer), circulation, the preparation of bulletin boards, the mending of books, and the preparation of overdue lists or notes. Volunteer parents can do many of these things but will require some training. (A letter of invitation for parent volunteers is included in Chapter 6.) Students are often willing helpers. Fourth through sixth grade students can be both conscientious and efficient. They are able to do such things as shelving, running errands, taking down bulletin boards, and assisting younger students to find books or to use equipment. They also enjoy pasting pockets in books, washing tables, and generally helping to keep the library neat. A Student Library Assistant Application is included here.

Some tasks are best reserved for you. These include budgeting, ordering, previewing materials, filling teacher requests, and planning.

The more efficiently you can manage your LMC, the more effective your program will be. Careful planning for the management of your LMC is time well spent.

STUDENT LIBRARY ASSISTANT APPLICATION

Student assistants in the LMC are very helpful to our library program. As an assistant you will be doing such things as putting books on the shelves, helping with bulletin boards, running errands, helping younger students, and doing other tasks that the librarian will assign to you from time to time.

Library assistants work before school and during recess times.

If you would like to be a library assistant, please fill out the application form below and return it to the LMC.

- -

STUDENT LIBRARY ASSISTANT APPLICATION

Name: _____ Grade: _____

I would like to be a library assistant because _____

_____.

I would be willing to do all the tasks assigned to me and I would try to be reliable.

The best time for me to work would be _____ before school _____ at recess.

Teacher Signature: _____

Parent Signature: _____

CIRCULATION MANAGEMENT

Checkout

Our most important concern is that books and other materials are being used. We do not want books resting neatly on the shelf; we want them circulating!

Checking the books out is the easy part of circulation — and there are many ways to manage it. Perhaps your library is automated and your checkout procedure is efficiently managed by computer. There are many types of computer systems that will be addressed more fully in another chapter.

If you are not yet computerized, there are many types of manageable circulation systems. Some librarians like to have the students' checkout cards kept in a folder or notebook. These notebooks can be kept either in the library or in the classroom. When kept in the classroom, the students (with teacher supervision) can put the cards back in the books to be returned before coming to the LMC. This leaves more time for your storytimes and for checkout. This system is probably best for younger children in grades kindergarten to grade three because it gives teachers closer control of the types of books read by the

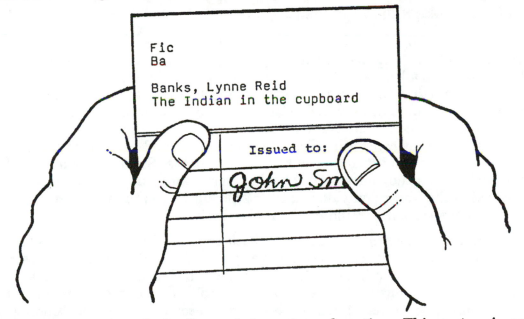

children and whether the books are being returned on time. This system is not advisable for older students, who tend to be careless with the cards.

A system for older students that requires less supervision than a regular checkout at the circulation desk is to have students write their name, grade, and the due date on the card and then write the due date on the date due slip in the book. The cards are then placed in a box on the checkout desk. The advantage to this system is that students can fill in the cards at a table rather than at the checkout desk, which sometimes becomes crowded. Another advantage is that students need not wait for the book and card to be stamped by a librarian. The traditional system requires the student to bring the book with his/her name and grade filled out on the card. The librarian then stamps the card and the book's date due slip with the due date. Cards in both systems are filed by the date due in call number order.

Often certain books are in great demand. To ensure a fair method of getting these books to the students who need them, devise some system of reserving books. Without a computerized system, you may use a spiral-bound lined book in which students could sign their names under the name of the book to be reserved. Computer systems have their own record-keeping system for reserving books. This is very effective because when the book comes back, the computer tells you that the book is on reserve and the name of the person who wants it. Without a computer, the book could be marked with a small colored label so that you or your assistants will recognize it as a reserved book whenever it is returned. In either system, hold the book for the person next in line. Have a special place for these books, and put a bookmark with the reserving student's name in the book and inform the students when it is their turn for a reserved book. A form for student notification of a reserved book is included at the end of this chapter.

Returning Materials to the LMC

Having books returned in a timely manner is important with these reserved books as with all books. You can help ensure the timely return of books by setting a practical limit on the number of books that can be checked out. The number of books allowed will depend on your collection and on how often students are allowed in the library. Ideally, they would be allowed to come in often so that they can return books they have read and select new ones. If this is possible, you can set a limit of two to three books. Students then can return the books when they have read them before checking out more. If students are allowed in the library only during their scheduled class time (not an ideal situation), many students would need a higher limit.

Incentives for bringing the books back are sometimes effective. Some possible incentives are special bookmarks or pencils for each student in classrooms that have no overdue books, a banner (sample included) to be displayed for a month by classrooms that have no overdue books, or a popsicle party for these classrooms. The principal can make an announcement each month listing the classes with no overdue books.

Regular overdue notes are probably the biggest help in getting books returned. Computerized systems will print these notes for you. In non-computerized LMCs, student library assistants can fill out the overdue notes for you. They also like to deliver these notes to the classrooms. (Some sample overdue notes are included.) Prior to sending overdue notices, a warning note can be sent to the classrooms. This note often brings in many books, saving hours of time writing overdue notes to the students.

How to Recover Books

With the price of books constantly increasing, it is important to avoid the needless loss of books. Often books are not returned when students leave the school during the year. The chances of getting books back from a student who has moved to another school are not good. The media specialist needs to be informed before students leave so she can check to see whether the departing student still has books signed out. Each classrooom teacher should be supplied with forms that can be filled out and sent to the LMC when a student is leaving. The media specialist then checks her records to see if the student has any library books out and then returns the filled-out note to the teacher. (A sample form is included.)

If the child leaves without returning the book or books, a note can be sent to the student's new school requesting the return of the books. Sometimes this helps, but it is better to get the books returned before the student leaves. (See sample letter.)

When a library book is a month or two overdue, a letter should be sent to the parents asking for the return of the book or payment for the book. Letters also should be sent if a book is damaged beyond repair. (Sample letters are included.)

At the end of the school year it is important to begin getting the books back well before the last day of school. Unless you have a very small school, you will probably need to close a week or two before the end of the school year to get the books returned and shelved. Set a date when all books are due and post signs around the school to remind the students (A sample poster is included.) After this date, send to each teacher a list of students who still have books checked out. If books are not returned a week before school is out, send bills to the parents or use the regular overdue letter. (Of course, computerized systems can generate these forms and teacher lists of still checked-out materials.)

PLEASE RESERVE...

_____
(Title)

For:

_____
(Student)

_____
(Grade)

HI! _____, _____
(Student)   (Grade)

YOU'RE IN LUCK! YOUR BOOK

_____

IS HERE!

Please come to the library and get it as soon as possible.

(Notes for Reserving Books)

GREAT JOB!

THIS CLASS HAD NO OVERDUE BOOKS LAST MONTH!

REMINDER

OVERDUE NOTICES WILL BE SENT OUT ON _____.

STUDENTS SHOULD RETURN ALL OVERDUE MATERIALS <u>NOW</u> AND TRY FOR THE PRIZE!

DID YOU FORGET?

You checked out the following:

_____

It was due _____.

Please return as soon as possible.

(Sample Banner and Sample Overdue Notes — Enlarge banner to appropriate size)

STUDENT WITHDRAWAL FROM SCHOOL FORM

TO THE LMC:

_____ will be leaving our school on

_____ and will be enrolled in _____School

in _____, _____. Please check your records and see

if there are any books still checked out to this student. Thank you.

_____, Teacher

_____

FROM THE LMC: All checked-out materials are returned _____

The following materials are still checked out _____

_____

_____

_____, Librarian

(Sample Forms for Students Leaving During School Year)

_____

_____

_____

_____ (Date)

Dear _____:

_____, a former student in our school, has entered your

school.

He/she forgot to return the following items to our LMC before leaving.

_____

_____

_____

_____

Would you please ask that these materials be returned to us? If the student returns them to

you, we would be happy to pay the postage for their return.

Thank you very much.

Sincerely,

_____, Librarian

(Sample Letter Sent to Another School After a Student Withdraws — Copy on School Letterhead)

_____ (Date)

Dear Parents of _____,

_____ has the following materials checked out from our school library.

Title: Date Due: Price:

_____ _____ _____

_____ _____ _____

_____ _____ _____

_____ _____ _____

Will you please help your child locate these materials and return them to the library as soon as possible? If they cannot be found, please note the price indicated for each item. If the materials are paid for and later found, your money will be refunded.

Thank you.

Sincerely,

_____, Librarian

(Sample Letter to Parents for Long-Overdue Books — Copy on School Letterhead)

_____ (Date)

Dear Parents of _____,

The following item _____, checked out by your child,

_____, has been damaged beyond repair and is no longer

suitable for circulation. We feel that our students should be responsible for material checked

out from our library.

In order that another copy of this book may be purchased for use in our library, we feel it is

necessary to request payment of $ _____ to cover the cost of replacement.

Please help us keep our collection complete.

Thank you.

Sincerely,

_____, Librarian

(Sample Letter to Parents for Damaged Books — Copy on School Letterhead)

AN ELEPHANT NEVER FORGETS!

ALL LIBRARY BOOKS ARE DUE BY
JUNE 1!

(Sample Poster for End-of-the-Year Book Returns — Enlarge to Appropriate Size)

Chapter Two

SUCCESSFUL DISCIPLINE

Achieving good discipline is not something we like to think about, but without it there can be no workable program in your LMC. The following are some guidelines and ideas for fostering a well-disciplined, happy library program and media center.

1. Good room arrangement
2. Challenging, well-planned program
3. Workable plan for good LMC conduct
4. Working with staff on your discipline plan
5. Discipline plan for your substitute

ROOM ARRANGEMENT

Make your LMC an inviting place, full of challenging activities that encourage children to participate in a variety of interesting choices. Areas in the LMC where students can read quietly are important, but it is also important to have areas where children can explore audiovisual materials such as sound filmstrips, videos, and computers. An area where students can quietly play mind-challenging games is also an asset. Providing various contests or voluntary research projects is a good idea, too.

In order to have all of the above available to children and still have a workable media center, careful room arrangement planning must be done. Have activity areas located away from the reference section or other areas that require concentration. For further information, see Chapter One for suggestions on the placement of various activity centers. Attention to the details of a well-planned room arrangement will do much to foster good discipline in your LMC.

A CHALLENGING PROGRAM

If students are presented with well-planned and interesting library skills programs as well as storytimes that are attention-grabbing and suited to their age level, they will have little opportunity or desire to misbehave.

Plan your library skills programs with as many hands-on activities as possible. For instance, students respond better to learning call numbers and book location if they locate actual books on the shelf rather than sorting books alphabetically by call number on a worksheet. Card catalog skills, also, are learned more quickly if each child is able to actually work with the cards in the card catalog rather than with a pictured card on a worksheet. Library skill games and literature appreciation sessions alternating with library skills sessions add interest for the students and contribute to their eagerness and desire to come to the LMC. (See Chapter 5 for specific ideas for teaching library skills.)

Storytimes are usually greatly anticipated by primary grade students. Plan simple opening activities that both entertain and serve to quiet the group and put them in a receptive frame of mind for the story. Here are some effective activities for you to try:

- Play 20 questions with an object in a treasure box, a sack, or even your pocket.
- Try to have the object related somehow to the story. A small toy elephant for *Horton Hatches the Egg* or a polished red stone for *Sylvester and the Magic Pebble*.
- Use a song, a finger play, or a riddle for useful attention grabbers.

Be sure the story is suitable for the age of the audience and exciting enough to hold the children's attention throughout. Watch for signs of restlessness, and be ready to give the students a stretch-and-wiggle break.

When the story is finished, establish a behavior routine for both checkout time and what students will do after checkout. Students who have returned their books and want to take out more must first find their books and then check them out before doing anything else. Establish with the teacher what they are to do after checkout. In some cases teachers prefer the child to return to the classroom directly after checkout and to sit down and read his/her book until the entire class has returned. Other teachers prefer that the students remain in the LMC for the entire period and return to the class as a group. If this is the case, it is advisable to have a set procedure for the students to follow after checkout. Establish a specific area where they are to go to look at their books. It should be a comfortable, attractive place with sufficient room for all the students. It may be a spot with comfortable cushions, rocking chairs, or a cozy couch. If you have stuffed animal or book characters there too, young students may wish to hold one and read to it while waiting to return to their classroom. Students who have overdue books and cannot check out any more could have a table to sit where there are pop-up books, flip books, and so on, which they may look at while waiting.

A WORKABLE PLAN FOR LMC CONDUCT

Before the start of the school year, be sure to have a discipline plan for your LMC. Knowing exactly what you will do in any given situation gives you a sense of security and enables students to feel comfortable in knowing your expectations. Plan to handle discipline yourself. Sending students to the principal should be resorted to only in the most severe circumstances. The students must know that you are in charge and that you expect them to be well-behaved in the LMC.

Although each school may have specific rules for their LMC, there are some universal ones practiced by most, such as using quiet voices, no running, putting away materials, and showing consideration to staff and other students. Even though the rules are clearly understood by the students, there will be times when infractions will occur. Be prepared with your own plan for consequences for disruptive students. Often a simple reminder is enough. Those students who persist might be sent back to their classroom. (Discuss this plan with teachers early in the school year.) In a case where a student is sent back to the room, he/she should be given a note to give to the classroom teacher. (A sample is included here.)

A note for the teacher letting him/her know when a class has done an especially good job is helpful and appreciated. This note can also be used to let the teacher know the skill or literature appreciation activity that occurred in the session.

A reward system of discipline is sometimes effective, especially with the upper grade students. In this system you might post a chart that lists each class. Whenever the class does well during their library time, a star is put on the chart. When the class has had four or five stars, reward them with a class session in which they may play the library games, watch a video, or use other audiovisual equipment. (A sample form is included for you).

Whether you use a reward system or another plan, consistency is the basis of good discipline in your LMC.

_____

is being sent back to class
because of refusal to follow
LMC rules.

_____
(Librarian)

did a **SUPER**
job in the LMC today!

_____
(Librarian)

Just to let
you know!

LIBRARY SKILLS

Class: _____

Skill covered:

_____ Reference

_____ Dewey Decimal System

_____ Literature appreciation

Comment:

_____
(Librarian)

Just to let you
know about

STORYTIMES

Class: _____

Story read:

Comment:

_____
(Librarian)

(Notes for Classroom Teacher)

GOOD JOB CHART!

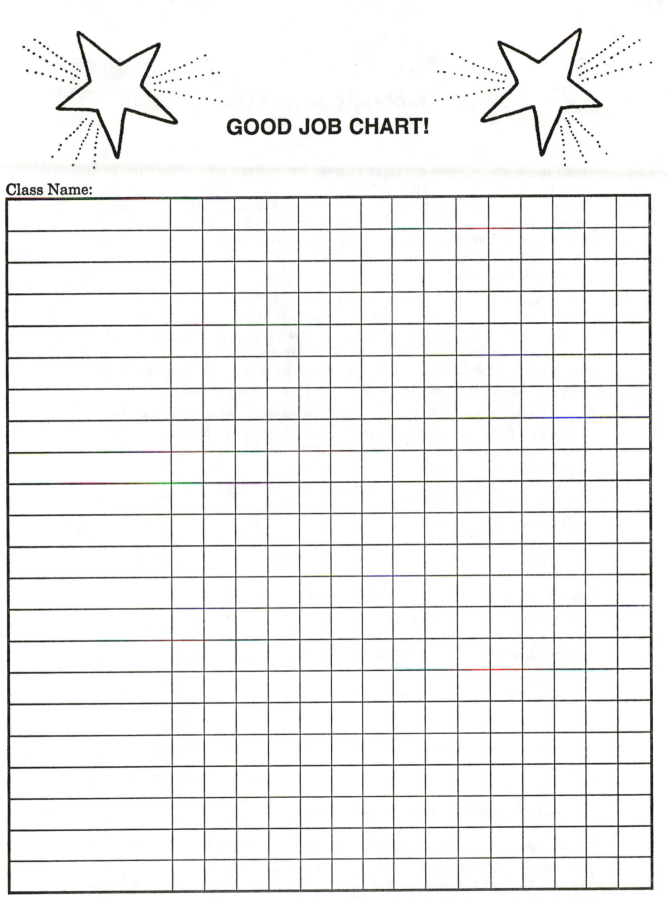

Class Name:

Put a star in a square for each time the class does a good job during a class session.

WORKING WITH STAFF ON YOUR DISCIPLINE PLAN

Whenever possible your discipline plan should coordinate with any school-wide plan in effect. If your school is following a reward-type plan such as positive action, be sure to award tokens to classes displaying appropriate conduct. If there is no building plan, make sure that your plan is explained to the teachers. They need to know that students may be sent back to the classroom for improper behavior. Before the start of school give them copies of the notes that you plan to use to indicate individual or classroom behavior. (See sample notes in this chapter.)

From the outset of the school year make it clear to teachers that the library is not a place for punishment for their students. The LMC should be an inviting, enjoyable place for them that fosters a love of learning and reading. Most children find the LMC to be a friendly and inviting place. By agreeing to let it be used for detention or for punishment defeats the purpose of creating a love of learning and an enjoyment of reading in our students.

Teachers can be a big help in establishing good discipline in the LMC early in the school year. Ideally, teachers should come with their classes and stay to help the students choose interesting books. Teachers are more aware of the individual reading abilities of their students and can help them find appropriate books. They also can help assure that each child learns appropriate LMC behavior. It is not likely, however, that the teachers will accompany their classes and remain the entire time during every LMC period for the whole year. In many schools teachers view this time as a preparation period. Plan with the teachers that they accompany their classes for the first two or three weeks, at least, for this will ensure that students will establish good habits in the LMC. It also gives teachers a better concept of your overall plan for their classes.

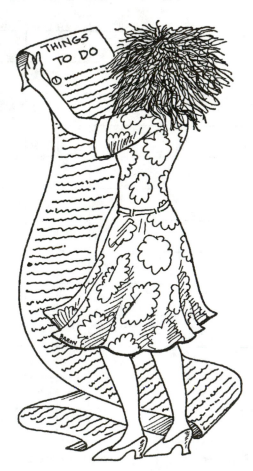

A sense of routine is important as students learn LMC conduct, and teachers can be of tremendous help in establishing it. Kindergarten and first-grade teachers are especially important in establishing a pattern of good behavior in the LMC that will probably continue throughout their school years.

After a few weeks, it is not quite as important that teachers remain with their classes. However, for special research the teacher should always plan to stay with his/her class.

A DISCIPLINE PLAN FOR YOUR SUBSTITUTE

To be sure that good discipline is maintained even in your absence, be sure your discipline plan is outlined for your substitute. Good lesson plans and a complete schedule help the substitute feel confident and in control. An outline of what you do to maintain discipline will also be of help. Be sure both your discipline plan and your lesson plans are clearly visible on your desk along with any books or other materials your substitute needs to carry out your plans. A sample form is included here. Adapt it to your own particular situation or make your own.

Dear Substitute,

    Thank you for coming today. I hope you will enjoy our LMC and our students. Here is the schedule for today and my discipline plan.

TIME	CLASS	ACTIVITY	MATERIALS/BOOKS

Your lunch time is: _____ Duties: _____

My Discipline Plan: _____

_____

_____

(Librarian)

(Schedule and Discipline Plan for Your Substitute)

© 1993 by The Center for Applied Research in Education

Chapter Three

READING PROMOTIONS

MY STATE READING CLUB

OVER THE RAINBOW READING

JOHNNY APPLESEED READING

READ FOR FUN!

SPECIAL READING PROMOTIONS

Helping children to become life-long readers is one of the most important responsibilities of an elementary school librarian. Although interesting storytimes and book talks help instill a joy for reading, special reading incentive programs are also helpful in motivating students to read. At times you may wish to plan and implement your own reading program especially fitted to your students, whereas at other times you may wish to make use of commercial reading programs.

Commercial Reading Programs

There are many commercial reading programs available. Some are run by the local franchise of national companies and offer reading incentive prizes at no expense to you. The reading programs run by Pizza Hut, Easter Seal's Readathon, and World Book's Partners in Excellence are examples of this type. Addresses for these programs are at the end of this chapter.

There are other reading programs that may be purchased. Junior Great Books is one of these programs. This is a reading program that offers no prize-type incentives. It is a program in which students read great literature and then discuss it in depth with an adult leader. In this program the books are purchased and the leaders must be trained.

Another purchased program that does provide incentives through prizes is Books and Beyond. This program has several themes, such as "Jogging Across the U.S.A.," "Travel in Time," "Treasures of the Deep," and "Around the World." The students read enough books to reach eight different levels and receive a prize at each level. When students achieve the eighth level, they receive a gold medal at a special assembly. This is a worthwhile program since children are often excited about it, but it requires a great deal of work and the assistance of many parent volunteers.

UPSTART and DEMCO both offer theme-centered reading programs that may be purchased. They also have reading activities and programs related to National Children's Book Week and National Library Week.

Many reading programs are also available in book forms, such as the reading bingos found in *Reading Bingos, Puzzles and Research Activities for the Elementary School Year*. After using some of these, you can make up your own reading bingos. An Authors' Birthday Reading Club is outlined in *The New Elementary School Librarian's Almanac*. Both are available from the Center for Applied Research in Education.

Other reading programs are offered in *Readers' Clubhouse—Organized Reading Programs With a Purpose* by Jan Grubb Philpot, Incentive Publications, and *Celebrate With Books* by Imogene Forte and Joy MacKenzie, also published by Incentive Publications. *Accelerated Readers* is a computerized reading program in which children are encouraged to read old and new classics.

Your Own Reading Programs

You will probably be able to think up many reading programs of your own, and these are especially useful because they will reflect the interests and abilities of your own particular student population. Presented here are three successful reading promotions to help you build programs of your own.

"My State" Reading Promotion

"My State" Reading Club is a program that would be especially useful during the month of your state's admission into the Union.

Put up a big map of your state on a large bulletin board in the LMC. On the map mark points of interest and major cities. Number each of the cities and interest points. Have each participating student put his/her name on a bicycle (pattern is given on page 42) and begin at your own city or town. You may have them progress on the map by number of minutes read or by number of books read. Students may also be given a map on which they can record their progress by drawing a line from city to city or point of interest. To get to the first stop in the reading program students should read a book about their own state — either fiction or nonfiction.

A sample form on which students may record their progress is given for the state of Oregon. Devise your own for your particular state. A note is also included for parents to sign that the student has read the book to them or read it silently and then discussed it with them.

Suitable prizes for this reading program might be pencils with your state name on them; an appropriate bookmark (one with a car or other vehicle); a state road map; or a car, airplane, or train eraser or pencil topper. Each student who completes the reading program should also receive a certificate, possibly in the shape of your state. (A sample is included.)

There are any number of activities that could go on at the LMC in conjunction with this reading program. Consider some of the following ideas.

Have a contest in which students memorize the counties in your state. When the student has memorized them all, that student could come to you and name the counties. Then the child's name is placed on a special bulletin board with a title appropriate for your state, such as: Who Knows Our Hoosier State? for Indiana students, Keen About Kentucky, Smart about South Dakota (or South Carolina), and so on.

Invite someone who is knowledgeable about your state to speak to your students about the history of the state, its scenic treasures, or the famous people who originated there. Another activity involves asking students to make posters advertising your state. Hang the poster in the LMC or in the hallway leading to the LMC. A sign saying "Read About Our State With a Book from Your Library" could accompany the posters.

Set up a research bulletin board with cutout pictures of different places in your state and have students identify the place by solving clues using latitude and longitude or names of famous people who were born there. When students solve the research questions, have their pictures mounted on a star and put on the bulletin board.

_____

(Name)

has read the book:

_____

(Title of Book)

_____

(Parent Signature)

_____

(Date)

_____

(Name)

has read the book:

_____

(Title of Book)

_____

(Parent Signature)

_____

(Date)

I LOVE MY STATE

I LOVE MY STATE

I LOVE MY STATE

I LOVE MY STATE

(Sample Forms for "My State Reading Club" — Parent's Notes Confirming the Student's Reading and Sample Bookmarks)

MY STATE READING CLUB
CERTIFICATE

_____

has read _____ books in the My State Reading Club program.

_____, Librarian

Date: _____

(Bicycle Patterns for Recording Students' Progress)

Student Record Sheet for My State Reading Club

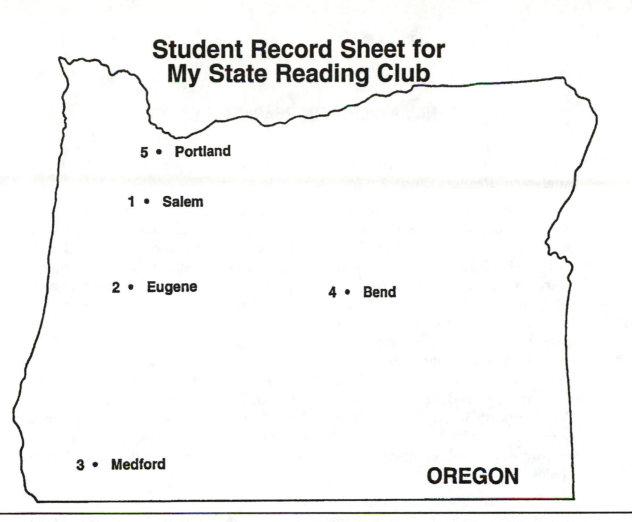

5 • Portland

1 • Salem

2 • Eugene

4 • Bend

3 • Medford

OREGON

Travel directions for My State Reading Club: Begin at city number 1 when you complete your first book. Draw a line to city number 2 when you read your second book, and then continue on until you reach our state's capital city, where your bicycle trip is completed. Record the titles and authors of your books on the lines below.

_____   _____

_____   _____

_____   _____

_____   _____

_____   _____

(Student Record Sheet for My State Reading Club)

"JOHNNY APPLESEED" READING PROMOTION

An enjoyable reading club for September or early fall is the "Johnny Appleseed" Readers Club.

Cover a large bulletin board with sky-blue paper. Enlarge the tree pattern to an appropriate size and place on the bulletin board. Add the enlarged figure of Johnny Appleseed to the bulletin board and space the words THE JOHNNY APPLESEED READERS at the top. (If you have an especially large bulletin board, you might put on a tree for each grade.) Print enough red apples, using the included pattern, for your student population. Student library aides or parent volunteers could cut out these apples. Tell the students that they will be given one of these paper apples to place on the tree each time they have spent an hour of recreational reading at home. Students who read the required number of hours will receive a Johnny Appleseed certificate and be invited to a party in the LMC. (If you prefer, a prize can be given rather than a party.) Possible party ideas could be treats of apple juice and popcorn or applesauce cookies and milk. Activities could be bobbing for apples, showing the movie of Johnny Appleseed, or having a local juggler teach the students how to juggle apples.

There are a number of apple activities you could use in conjunction with this reading program. For example, you could have students use the Apple Book Finders (included in this book) to find books on the shelves. This activity is good for third- and fourth-graders. Making apple dolls, cutting an apple and making prints with it, writing poetry about apples, researching Johnny Appleseed, and an apple research scavenger hunt (included in this book) are additional projects. Stories about Johnny Appleseed could be read during story times. *The Seasons of Arnold's Apple Tree* by Gail Gibbons is another possible storytime treat.

Dear Parents:

Your child is invited to participate in our Johnny Appleseed Readers Club Promotion. The purpose of this program is to encourage recreational reading. Whenever your child has read for 1 hour, please sign one of the notes below and have your child return it to the library. (Please notice that the bottom note is number 1 so that you may cut it off first.) Each time your child returns one of these notes, he/she will get to put an apple on our Johnny Appleseed tree. This reading program will run from _____ to _____. Children who read a total of five hours during this time will receive a Johnny Appleseed certificate and be invited to a Johnny Appleseed party.

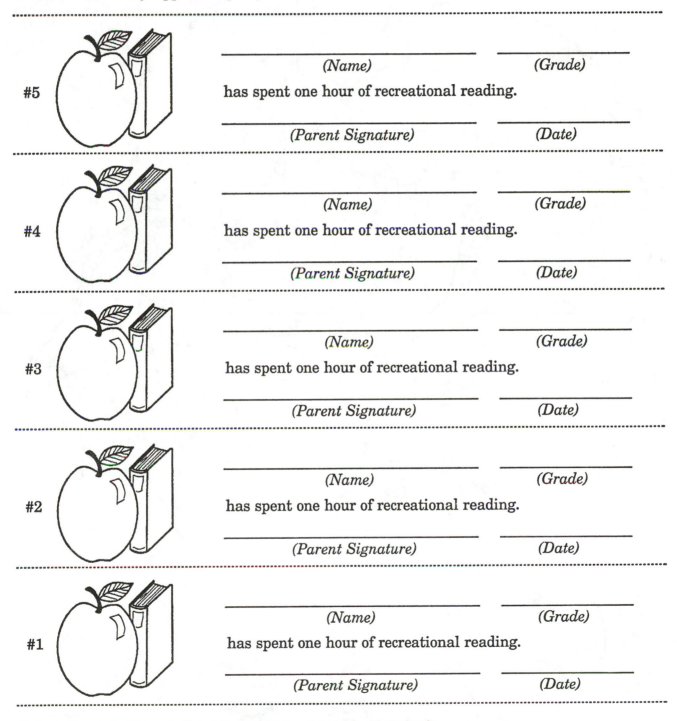

#5

_____ _____
(Name)   (Grade)
has spent one hour of recreational reading.

_____ _____
(Parent Signature)   (Date)

#4

_____ _____
(Name)   (Grade)
has spent one hour of recreational reading.

_____ _____
(Parent Signature)   (Date)

#3

_____ _____
(Name)   (Grade)
has spent one hour of recreational reading.

_____ _____
(Parent Signature)   (Date)

#2

_____ _____
(Name)   (Grade)
has spent one hour of recreational reading.

_____ _____
(Parent Signature)   (Date)

#1

_____ _____
(Name)   (Grade)
has spent one hour of recreational reading.

_____ _____
(Parent Signature)   (Date)

(Letter to Parents for Johnny Appleseed Reading Club — Put on School Letterhead)

Bulletin Board Patterns for the
Johnny Appleseed Readers Club

Enlarge the tree and Johnny Appleseed to fit the size of your bulletin board. Reduce the size of the apple to an appropriate size for your tree.

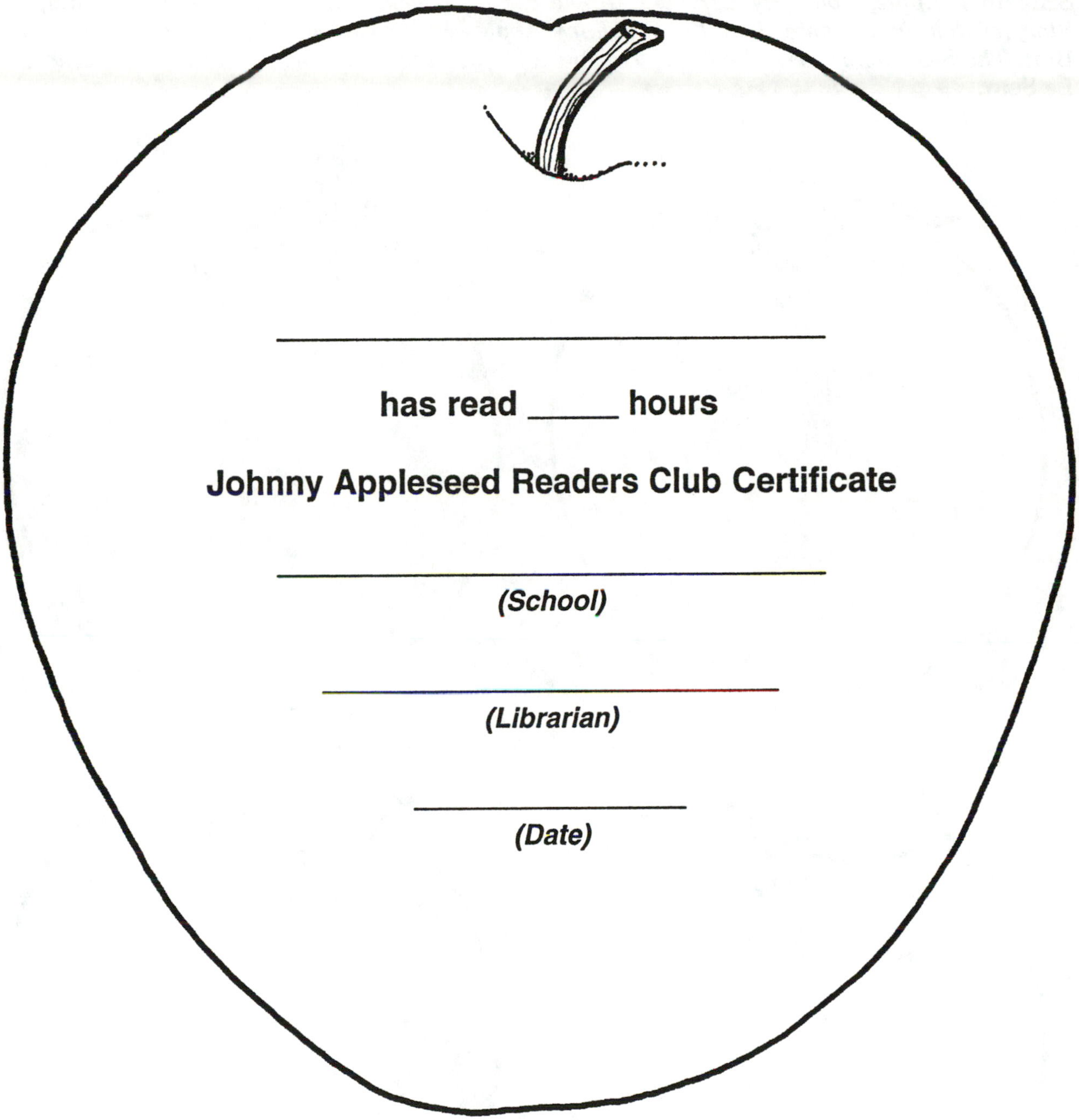

_____

has read _____ hours

Johnny Appleseed Readers Club Certificate

_____

(School)

_____

(Librarian)

_____

(Date)

(Print this certificate on bright-red paper. Have volunteers cut out the apple-shaped certificates.)

Apple Book Finders

Copy the patterns below on bright-red paper. Put the title and call number of an apple book on each cutout pattern. Laminate for sturdiness and let students find the titles on the shelves. Possible titles are *Applebet* by Watson, *An Apple Tree Through the Year* by Schneiper, *Apple Mouse* by Ulrich, *A, Apple Pie* by Greenaway, *Apples* by Hogrogrian, *The Story of Johnny Appleseed* by Aliki, *Johnny Appleseed* by Kellogg, *Apple and the Arrow* by Buff, *The Seasons of Arnold's Apple Tree* by Gibbons, and *Little Brother of the Wilderness* by Le Seur.

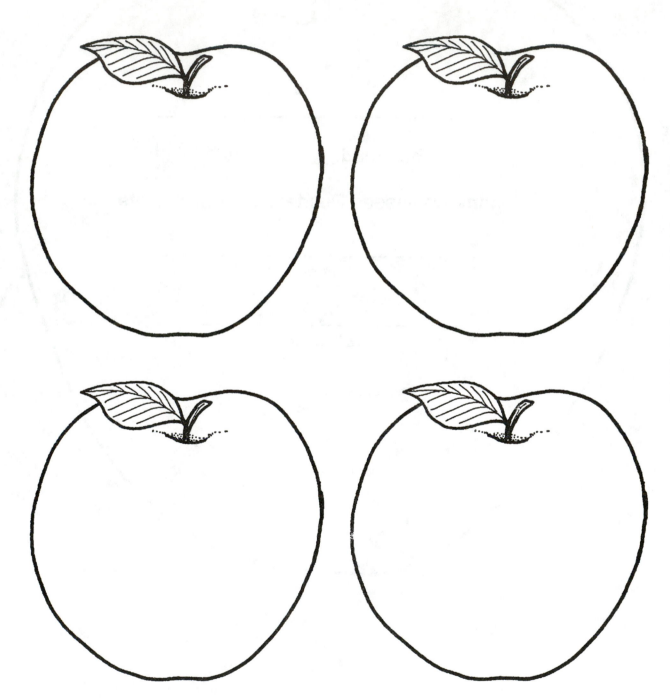

Name: _____   Grade: _____

Apple Scavenger Hunt

1. Look up the word **apple** in an encyclopedia. Name three different kinds of apples.

   _____   _____   _____

2. Using the geographical dictionary, tell in which state Apple Valley is located. _____

3. Using the biographical dictionary, find out why John Francis Appleby is famous._____

4. Apples are delicious. Use the thesaurus to find another word that means "delicious."_____

5. Does your library have books about apples? Use the card catalog to find the titles and call numbers of two books about apples.

   _____ Call number: _____

   _____ Call number: _____

"READ ALONG THE RAINBOW ROAD" READING PROMOTION

An appropriate reading club for spring is a "Read Along the Rainbow Road" Reading Club. By now first graders are becoming good readers, so that they, too, may take part in this reading program.

In this reading program students earn a reading certificate by choosing to read at home a total of 8 hours during the designated month. (April is an appropriate month because May often has too many end-of-the-year activities.)

Prepare a bulletin board to advertise the club and to record the names of the "pot-of-gold" readers. The bulletin board looks best with a sky-blue background featuring a colorful rainbow. At the end of the rainbow place a large pot of gold. As children complete the required number of hours of reading, their names can be placed on this pot of gold. Cut out large letters for the caption, "Read Along the Rainbow Road." (See the bulletin board suggestion below.)

Introduce the reading club and explain the requirements. Explain that all who complete the reading will receive a bag of gold coins (gold-wrapped chocolate coins). They will also each receive a certificate — and their name will be placed on the bulletin board pot of gold.

Patterns for Read Along the Rainbow Road Bulletin Board — Enlarge to fit your bulletin board

READ ALONG THE RAINBOW ROAD READING CLUB

A Note to Parents: This reading program is designed to encourage greater recreational at-home reading by our students. Every time your child spends time at home reading for fun (not for schoolwork), that time is recorded on this sheet. Cooperation between parent and child is helpful in recording and totaling the time on the calendar below. (Credit may also be given for the time parents spend reading to their children.) When the student accumulates the required time, return the bottom portion of this page to the library. A certificate and a "bag of gold" (gold-covered chocolate coins) will be awarded to each reader.

Name: _____ Grade: _____

Month: _____

SUN.	MON.	TUE.	WED.	THU.	FRI.	SAT.

© 1993 by The Center for Applied Research in Education

Time: _____ Parent Signature: _____

(Record Sheet for the Read Along the Rainbow Road Reading Promotion —
Put the correct dates in the month pattern on student record sheet)

has completed the requirements for

Read Along the Rainbow Readers Club Certificate

(School)

(Librarian)

(Date)

(Copy This Certificate on Gold-Colored Paper)

Card Catalog Capers for Use With the Rainbow Reading Promotion

Put the following titles, or other "colorful" titles, on the rainbow patterns below. Glue or tape the patterns onto tongue depressor sticks. The sticks can be placed in a bright-colored container and placed on top of the card catalog. Students in third and fourth grade classes can each be given a title to look up in the card catalog. (Try to use titles from as many different drawers as possible.) Students may use the tongue depressors as markers to mark the place where their title is found. They should then be ready to answer questions about the card.

Some possible titles are *A Rainbow of My Own, Blue Willow, A Color of His Own, Green Eggs and Ham, Orange Oliver, Purple Pussycat, The Red Balloon, Yellow House Mystery, Dragons of Blueland, Calico Cat Looks at Colors, Amy Loves the Rain,* etc.

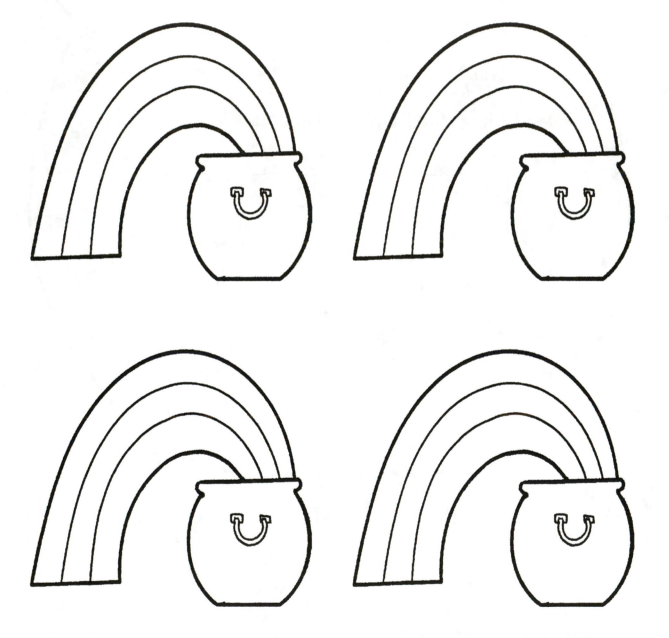

Rainbow Shelf Search

Name: _____ Date: _____ Grade: _____

Look in the Fiction Section and find a book for each of the following rainbow colors.

Write the title and the author for each.

Color:	Title:	Author:
Red	_____	_____
Orange	_____	_____
Yellow	_____	_____
Green	_____	_____
Blue	_____	_____
Purple	_____	_____

ADVERTISING BOOKS AND READING

One of the important jobs of a media specialist/librarian is promoting and advertising books and reading. Bulletin boards, bookmarks, book talks, storytimes, and activities with student involvement can all be used to promote books and reading. There are many commercial companies that sell book promotion materials, or you may find it fun to make your own. Some of these companies are UPSTART, DEMCO, ALA, and Highsmith. Their products are colorful and exciting, but your own promotions may be more suitable for your own particular students. Using themes throughout the year can tie your bulletin boards, bookmarks, and other promotional activities together.

Some possible themes are sports, dinosaurs, pets, pioneers, explorers, space, space travel, folk tales, holidays, poetry, patriotism, Pilgrims, minorities, and so forth. Planning your themes for the year gives you a framework from which to build. Look through catalogs and order materials that will enhance your themes. Plan activities for students that follow the theme. Bibliographies can be prepared on the themes. You can make your decisions as to which books you will use for storytimes and book talks based on the theme.

You can promote books and reading with various student activities, such as making bookmarks, voting for favorite books, making posters advertising favorite books, and preparing and acting in skits or puppet plays. You can also give a book talk or book suggestions through the intercom during morning announcements.

Students enjoy riddles about favorite books. Start with one clue and add a clue a day until many students have figured out the book title. For example, Day 1: An amphibian is the main character in this book. Day 2: This amphibian is bossy. Day 3: This amphibian thinks he is king of the pond. Day 4: This amphibian wants to be higher than any other animal. Day 5: This amphibian is no longer king after a little turtle burps. (*Yertle the Turtle* by Dr. Seuss) This riddle could be for all elementary school students. Another one for older students could be: Day 1: I live in Idaho. Day 2: My real name is Leroy. Day 3: I am good at solving mysteries. Day 4. The author of my book is Donald Sobol. Day 5: My last name is Brown. (*Encyclopedia Brown, Boy Detective* by Donald Sobol)

Students enjoy making up riddles about their favorite books. Have each of them make up a riddle and let the other students guess.

During Children's Book Week or National Library Week, older students could visit classrooms and perform a book rap. (This could also be used in a school assembly.) Students could make up their own or you could use the one on the next page.

Books, Books they're the best!

They'll get you through the toughest test!

They'll teach you how to make a kite!

And even how to fly it right!

They'll teach you how to play the game.

They'll teach you how the Pilgrims came.

They'll take you to another land

Of sunny beaches and golden sand.

They'll make you laugh, they'll make you cry,

And teach you how to make a pie!

They are your friends, so check them out!

You'll love what reading's all about!

Students are also capable of writing amusing limericks about favorite books or favorite characters. Teach them the form of a limerick and then give them an example, such as:

There once was a good bear named Pooh.

Piglet never knew what he would do.

Pooh loved eating honey,

And often was funny,

But Christopher Robin loved Pooh!

Addresses for Commercial Reading Promotions

BOOKS AND BEYOND
Solana Beach School District
309 N. Rios
Solana Beach, CA 92075

BOOKS ACROSS AMERICA
Solana Beach School District
309 N. Rios
Solana Beach, CA 92075

DEMCO
P.O. Box 7488
Madison, WI 53707-7488

WONDERSTORMS
1278 West Ninth Street
Cleveland, Ohio 44113

UPSTART
Box 889
Hagerstown, MD 21741

BOOK-IT
(Pizza Hut Reading Incentive Program)
1-800-4-BOOK-IT

WORLD BOOK PARTNERS IN EXCELLENCE
Contact World Book in State's Largest City
or Call 1-800-621-8202

Other companies offering reading programs:

Chapter Four

RUNNING SPECIAL PROGRAMS

Planning and implementing LMC programs with an emphasis on fun is one of the joys of being a librarian/media specialist. Special-interest centers, speakers, author visits, contests, displays, and exhibits all contribute to students' eager visits to the LMC and foster their joy for learning. Although you will find that many ideas will occur to you to enhance your special programs, here are some ideas that may help you get started.

EXHIBITS AND DISPLAYS

Students enjoy looking at exhibits and displays. You can exhibit collections from faculty, students, or community members. Exhibits that appeal to most students or that enhance a larger media center theme are especially appropriate. Examples of such exhibits are antique greeting cards for the various holidays, dolls from other countries, rocks, special buttons, election campaign buttons and signs, bookmark collections, antique books, baseball cards, coins, and certain hobbies.

Some of these exhibits may be very valuable and will need to be kept in a locked display case. Other exhibits may be less valuable and could even be accessible for students to handle. Be sure each exhibit is attractively displayed and labeled with the name of the owner.

Student Exhibits

One way to solicit student exhibits is to have a posted sign-up sheet in the LMC on which students can indicate the nature of their exhibit and the date when he/she would like to exhibit it in the LMC. A note can be sent to the student a week before the time for his/her exhibit and another note sent when it is time for the student to remove it from the LMC.

Name: _____

Grade: _____

You are scheduled to exhibit your collection of _____

in the LMC beginning _____.

We are looking forward to seeing your exhibit.

_____, Librarian

Name: _____

Grade: _____

It is time for you to remove your collection from the LMC. Please stop by after school and pick it up.

Thank you for sharing your interesting exhibit with us. Everyone enjoyed it.

_____, Librarian

(Sample Notes for Student Exhibits)

Exhibits From Parents and Faculty

Try to solicit exhibits from parents and faculty members by mentioning it in your school newspaper. A sample request for your paper might read something like the following:

Exhibits Wanted

The LMC is looking for interesting exhibits to display. Students enjoy collections of such things as rocks, cards, buttons, dolls, coins, and so on. If you have a collection or hobby that you would be willing to exhibit in our LMC, please contact me.

_____, Librarian

Again, be sure that exhibits are attractively displayed and safe from eager hands. When the exhibit has been removed, be sure to send a thank you note. A sample note follows.

T H A N K   Y O U !

Date: _____

Dear_____,

Thank you so much for sharing your _____ collection with us. The students and staff found it very interesting. We appreciate your willingness to share it with us.

_____, Librarian

SPEAKERS AND DEMONSTRATIONS

Authors and illustrators are favorite speakers in the LMC. It is important to schedule these speakers since children are inspired and motivated by them to wider reading choices and to greater creativity in writing and illustrating. The opportunity to interact with a real, live author provides students with very meaningful experiences.

Famous authors and illustrators may charge high fees for their programs, and they usually must be scheduled far in advance. However, if you are able to obtain the funding, they are well worth it. Perhaps you can set aside a fund in your general budget for these speakers. Many times parent-teacher groups are willing to pay for an author's or illustrator's program. Proceeds from your book fair can also be used for this purpose.

Sometimes you can find an author or illustrator who appeals to all ages of students. When this is not the case, try to schedule two author visits — one appropriate for younger students and another for the older students.

You can also look for new authors or illustrators in your immediate area who may be willing to come to your LMC for a small fee or none at all. If you are fortunate enough to locate someone like this, you may be able to have several authors/illustrators visit during the school year. Whenever a speaker is scheduled, be sure to make careful arrangements beforehand. Some things to consider: the fee, providing directions to your school, the appropriate grade levels for the presentation, the speaker's schedule, their special needs (P.A. system, special table, an easel, overhead, slide projector and screen), and lunch arrangements.

Be sure that students who will hear the speaker are well-prepared by having the teachers read one or more of the author's or illustrator's books. Try to borrow these books from other schools or public libraries when you do not have enough. Authors or illustrators may want to sell their books after their program. Make arrangements for this to be accomplished as smoothly as possible.

Authors and illustrators usually autograph any purchased books. They are usually unwilling to autograph scraps of paper, notebooks, and so on, which students may bring. Find out from the author before his/her visit whether autographs will be given. Make sure students understand the conditions for the signing. If the author is only willing to autograph a purchased book, you could make a bookmark that the author could autograph and then make copies of it for the students.

At some point during the visit, take pictures of the author/illustrator so you can display the photographs in the LMC as a reminder of this occasion. After the program, be sure to have the check ready for the author/illustrator.

Encourage students to write thank you notes to the author. Some students enjoy drawing pictures to include with their notes. Send these to the author along with your personal thank you.

Storytellers may also be willing to present a program in the LMC. The previous suggestions for authors are also appropriate for storytellers. You may be able to find willing storytellers in the community, at a local college, through the public library, or from a community theater group. High school drama groups are also a good source for storytellers. Often the local public librarian will be able to tell you the names of storytellers in your area. Professional storytellers, like famous authors, can charge high fees, but you can sometimes find good storytellers who will tell their stories for a small fee or none at all.

Storytellers often prefer small groups of children so that they can interact with them. Try to have small groups of children in a quiet informal setting for the storyteller. The gymnasium or cafeteria are usually too large and too noisy for good storytelling. Talk to your storyteller well in advance of the program so that you may find out the setting needed, the maximum number of children in each group, and the most suitable age group. After the storyteller has gone, children may want to draw pictures about the stories they have heard. These are appropriate to send to the storyteller along with your personal thank you and those of any appreciative teachers or students.

Follow these guidelines for other entertainers, such as puppeteers or mimes. Always plan with the entertainer well in advance to ensure an enjoyable experience for both the audience and the presenter.

FOCUS ON FUN

Encourage students to participate in library programs by providing many fun-to-do activities. These activities can focus on research, card catalog use, literature awareness, or just plain fun!

Autumn Fun

Let the students have fun getting acquainted with the teachers by matching a little-known fact about each teacher to the teacher's picture and name. Take a picture of each teacher and ask him/her for an interesting fact that students could enjoy knowing about that person. On a large bulletin board mount each teacher's picture on a bright-red paper apple with the teacher's name printed on it. Write the unknown facts about each teacher on yellow apples. A caption could be *Getting to Know Your Teachers*. Students are challenged to match the fact with the correct teacher by questioning the teachers. Provide an answer sheet for students to use which corresponds with the bulletin board. Award a small prize to the student matching the most names — a bright apple note pad, a back-to-school student supply box, a box of new pencils, or a book about teachers, such as *Miss Nelson Is Missing* by Harry Allard or *My Teacher Is an Alien* by Bruce Coville.

The teachers' pictures could be saved and used during the year for other bulletin boards, such as

- *Teachers' Pets* — Teachers supply a picture of his/her pet and students match the pet to the teacher.

- *You Must Have Been a Beautiful Baby* — Teachers bring a baby picture of themselves and students match the teacher to his/her baby picture.

- *Teachers' Favorite Hobby* — Teachers bring in examples of their hobby, such as a painting, a quilt, and so on, or something representing their hobby, such as ice skates for ice skating or ballet slippers for dancing. Mount the teacher's picture and name beside the hobby.

- Another way to encourage students to know the teachers is to take a picture of each teacher with their favorite childhood book. Ask each teacher to tell the name of the book and why they enjoyed it. This is appropriate for Children' Book Week in November or National Library Week in April.

A *Pumpkin Poetry Patch* bulletin board is fun to do in October. Encourage students to write a poem for autumn or Halloween. Type each poem and mount it on a bright-orange pumpkin, including the name of the poet. Each child writing a poem may put his/her name in a decorative pumpkin or jack o'lantern. At the end of the month, a drawing can be held. The person whose name is drawn can win a Pumpkin Patch Poetry Prize, which could be a popular poetry book, such as *Where the Sidewalk Ends* by Shel Silverstein or one of Jack Prelutsky's books. Other ideas for prizes could be a Halloween book, a

Halloween makeup kit, or a giant pumpkin. After the bulletin board is taken down, bind the poems, still mounted on the pumpkins, into a book titled *Pumpkin Patch Poetry*, which can then be checked out by the students.

Cat Week is celebrated in November. Cut out cat shapes and write the titles and call numbers of cat books on the shape. During class times let students find the books on the shelves. Enlarge the following cat shapes for this activity.

One creative-writing activity for November is to encourage students to write turkey tales. (A turkey pattern is provided.) Mount the stories on a bulletin board with a caption such as *Turkey Tales*. Later, bind the stories into a book for students to check out.

(Pattern for Turkey Tale Creative Writing)

Winter and Holiday Fun

A winter holiday activity that is colorful as well as enjoyable is a holiday "guesstimation" contest. Fill a big glass jar (a gallon jar from the cafeteria works well) with small Christmas ornaments. Fill a small jar with the same type of ornaments. Count the number in the smaller jar and put a sign near it saying, *There are _____ ornaments in this jar. Estimate the number in the large jar.*

Have supply forms like the one below placed near the jars for the students to use. The student estimating the number closest to the actual number can be awarded a small prize.

© 1993 by The Center for Applied Research in Education

HOLIDAY "GUESSTIMATION"

Name: _____

Grade: _____

My guess is _____ ornaments.

Another holiday idea is to wrap a paperback copy of a well-known children's book in holiday paper. Print a clue about the book each day until someone guesses the correct title. The first student to guess the title is given the book.

A similar idea is to wrap small empty boxes such as toothpaste boxes or small jewelry boxes in colorful holiday paper. On each wrapped box place a typed question about a Caldecott book, such as, "In what book do a brother and a sister discover a box in a park? They take the box home and play an interesting game." (*Jumanji* by Van Allsburg)

Other questions could be "In what book do a boy and his father go out on a snowy evening looking for a night creature?" (*Owl Moon* by Jane Yolen) or "In what book do a king and a queen invite a little boy to tea? (*May I Bring a Friend?* by DeRegniers) or "In what book does a girl meet eggs that talk and cows with two heads?" (*The Talking Eggs* by Robert San Souci)

Type questions for ten or more boxes and then place the brightly wrapped boxes in a basket. Students try to guess the names of the books. Each time they correctly guess the Caldecott title, give them a holiday sticker.

A free-time research activity for the holiday season is to have holiday questions and instructions printed on a cardboard ornament. Put the ornaments on a small Christmas tree. Children may take an ornament and try to answer the questions or follow the instructions by using various reference books. Each time they tell you a correct answer, give them a holiday sticker. They then return the ornament to the tree. (You may wish to color code your ornament questions by grade level.) The following are some possible questions/instructions and ornament patterns:

— Look up the word *snowfall* in the almanac. Where did the great blizzard of 1888 occur? (In the eastern United States. There were 400 deaths.)

— Find the fiction book *Snow Dog* by Kjelgaard. Show it to a librarian.

— Go to the nonfiction section and find a book on holidays. (394)

— Look up the word *snow* in the card catalog. What is the nonfiction number for snow? ( )

— Find the word *celebrate* in a thesaurus. Give one synonym for *celebrate*. (rejoice, commemorate, and so on — answers may vary)

— Look up the word *holidays* in the card catalog. What is the nonfiction number for *holidays*? (394)

— Using an encyclopedia, find out when the first Christmas card was created and where. (In 1843 — in England)

— What is another name for Hanukkah? (Festival of Lights)

— Use a biographical dictionary to look up Clement Clarke Moore. What Christmas story is he famous for? (*A Visit From St. Nicholas*, sometimes called *The Night Before Christmas*)

— Use *Bartlett's Familiar Quotations* to look up the word *Christmas*. Find one good Christmas quotation and read it to the librarian. (answers will vary)

— Use the *Guinness Book of World Records* to find out the height of the world's tallest Christmas tree. Where was it erected? (221 ft. Douglas fir in Seattle; may change in succeeding years!)

In February you can provide several presidential trivia activities, such as matching presidents with their nicknames, their slogans, or their first ladies. (You can find these and any other facts of this sort in the book *Facts About the Presidents*.)

February is also a good time to have a *Dress As Your Favorite Historical Character Day*. This activity comes after the biographies stressed during the month of February. Children and teachers who dress as a historical character could parade through the building, coming to the library last. In the library, take a picture of each person. These pictures could later be used on a bulletin board captioned, *Can You Guess the Names of the Historical Characters Pictured Here?*

Especially effective during Winter Olympic years, but usable at any time, are activities featuring winter sports. Display books on skiing, ice skating, sledding, and hockey on a large bulletin board with a snow-covered mountain and a skating pond. Caption the board *Pick a Winner*. Copy the figures and the sled below. Type questions about winter and winter sports on the back of the sled. Place these questions in a sleigh (available at after-Christmas sales) for students to draw from. After correctly answering them, they select one of the winter sports figures, write their name on it, and place it on the bulletin board. At the end of the month, invite all students whose names are on the bulletin board to a winter party. At the party serve popcorn and hot chocolate or hot cider. Show a video with a winter theme or provide games for small groups.

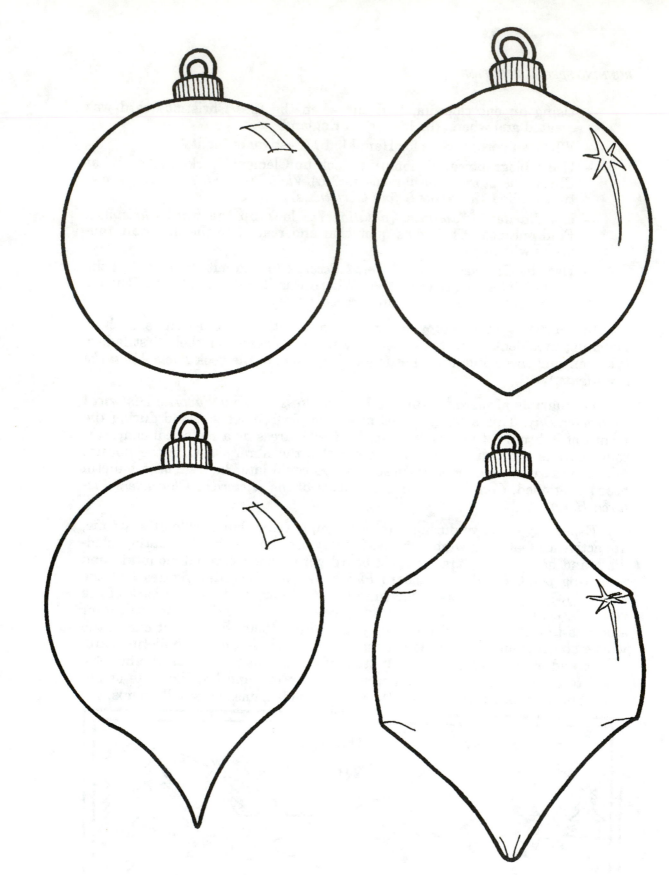

(Patterns for Question Ornaments)

(Patterns for "Pick A Winner" Winter Activity)

Spring Fun

The Easter Bunny Says activity is fun to use in the spring. Type as many instructions or questions which you will need for your students on small pieces of paper. Fold these and place in small bright-colored plastic eggs along with a jelly bean (one instruction and one jelly bean in each egg). Place these eggs in a large basket. Students choose an egg and then do the activity. When they have successfully completed the activity, they may eat the jelly bean. Here are some sample instructions/questions. (You should use different questions for different grade levels.)

— The Easter Bunny says, "Find a Caldecott book and turn to the title page. Raise your hand when you have found it." (Grades 2 and 3)

— The Easter Bunny says, "Find a book by Marc Brown. Raise your hand when you have found it." (Grades 2 and 3)

— The Easter Bunny says, "Find a book of fairy tales." (Grades 3 and 4)

— The Easter Bunny says, "Use the card catalog to find a book about Easter. Raise your hand and be ready to tell the copyright date, the title, the author, and the number of pages in the book." (Grades 3 to 5)

— The Easter Bunny says, "Where is Easter Island located?" (South Pacific Ocean — Grades 4 and 5)

— The Easter Bunny says, "Use the geographical dictionary to find out where Rabbit Ears Pass is located." (Colorado — Grades 4 to 6)

— The Easter Bunny says, "Use the biographical dictionary to find out why George Eastman was famous." (photography — Grades 4 to 6)

— The Easter Bunny says, "Use a book of quotations to find out who said, 'No sun upon an Easter day is half so fine a sight' ". (Sir John Suckling — Grades 5 and 6)

Vacation is Coming! Where Will Our Teachers Be? is a good activity for the end of the year. On a large bulletin board, make a colorful map of the world (or of North America if no one is traveling any farther than this). Ask each teacher where he/she will be going during the summer. Place each teacher's picture around the edge of the bulletin board. Place the caption above the bulletin board. Next to the bulletin board, place the activity sheets for the students to use. The activity sheet could read something like, *Mr. Jones will be in a state bordered by Canada, South Dakota, Montana, and Minnesota. Where will he be?* (in North Dakota), *Mrs. Smith will be in a state in which the Space Needle is located.* (Seattle, Washington), or *Mr. Brown will be in a country whose capital is Oslo.* (Norway). These questions will vary, depending on where each teacher is going. This activity could be done in a skills class or as a voluntary contest.

Any-Time-of-Year Activities

Keeping a school scrapbook of newspaper articles, snapshots of reading club parties, holiday parties, author visits, special award assemblies, teacher news, and so on provides much enjoyment. Students love to look at scrapbooks from the current and previous years. Keep the scrapbooks near a comfortable seating area so that children may enjoy them during their free time.

Additional interest centers can include:

- Art- or craft-oriented centers where students can learn origami or how to weave God's Eyes. Students or volunteer adults can instruct.

- A simple science experiment corner with an adult volunteer.

- A center with artifacts from a foreign country — if possible, with someone from that country who could explain the items to the students.

- A center promoting your state and featuring books, travel brochures, and a poster detailing free things to do in your state.

- A puppet place with a theater and puppets is a big hit with students.

Be Kind to Animals. They have a lot to say. What are these animals saying? is a popular and attractive bulletin board. Place several photographs of interesting-looking animals on the board. Let the students think of things the animals could be saying if the animals could talk. Place the best captions under the pictures.

Student Authors' Day

An entertaining and appropriate program for the LMC to sponsor is a student authors' day. On this day all students in the entire school will have an opportunity to share a book that they have written. To give the teachers and students ample time to produce these books, this program should be planned early in the year and the actual authors' day held late in the spring. There are many ways to carry out and plan for an authors' day. One way might be to exhibit the students' books at an evening open house. Invite a famous author as a guest for the evening to give writing tips to the students and to provide a question-and-answer session for them.

You could also plan a school-wide all-day student authors' day. This is an exciting experience for the students and well worth the tremendous effort it requires. Because of the amount of work involved, be sure to ask two or three staff members to help plan and organize your authors' day. Many volunteers also will be needed on the actual authors' day.

Plan to divide your student population into groups of ten students with one volunteer for each group. This volunteer will remain with her/his group for the entire day. If the group is of various grade levels, older students can be a buddy to kindergarten and first grade children.

On the actual day set up three or four stations throughout the school. Each group of ten students will visit each station some time during the day. The stations might be a place where the students sit with the group leader for one hour in order to read his or her book. After each reading, every member of the group tells something good about the story that was just read. The group leader writes down each positive statement on a special comment sheet along with the name of the commenting student. (See the sample comment sheet included here.) At another station could be a famous author. Students at this station could listen to the author tell about his/her books and then ask questions. At still another station could be a storyteller. A fourth station could be set up as an activity center where students would be able to choose one or two activities, such as making pop-up books, thumb-print books, accordion books, puppets, masks, and so on. Allow an hour for each station and an hour for the lunch period. If the authors' day is held in the spring, the lunch might be an outdoor picnic.

When planning, you must also divide the student groups into three (or four) larger groups — the number depends on how many stations you have. The name tags for the students should be color coded so they will know which group they are with. The tags should also have the group leader's name or number. On authors' day, the entire student body should gather in the auditorium or gymnasium, where they will hear their schedule. For example: All groups with the red designation might go to the author station; yellow might go to the storyteller; green to the activity center; blue would scatter to quiet corners in the school where they could read and critique their books.

Group leaders should be made up of as many members of the staff as possible, including teachers, assistants, principals, and secretaries. Many parent or community volunteers will also be needed. In addition to one group leader for each ten students, you will need volunteers for each activity center. Let each teacher be responsible for obtaining two or three volunteers. A training session for these volunteers should be held the evening before the student authors' day.

Before the day, prepare for each group leader a bag containing the following items for each child: a program, a comment sheet, a certificate to be given to the children at the day's end, and a plastic bag in which the student can keep his/her book, pencil, and completed activities. Also be sure that each of the leader's bags contains a hall pass in case someone in the group needs to use the restroom.

Name tags with group assignments could be given to each student in the classroom prior to the start of the activities. Use the following forms or make forms to suit your own situation.

GOOD JOB!

GOOD WORK!

_____ School
Student Authors' Day

_____ *(Date)*

Book Comment Sheet

by _____

Comment: Person Commenting:

_____   _____

_____   _____

_____   _____

_____   _____

_____   _____

_____   _____

_____   _____

_____   _____

_____   _____

_____

(Group Leader)

Autographs of Authors I Met Today

_____ School

Student Authors' Day

_____ (Date)

(Autograph-Signing Form — copy on parchment or similar paper and fold in the middle; student authors sign one another's program's.)
(Program Cover)

© 1993 by The Center for Applied Research in Education

STATION LOCATIONS

Storyteller: _____

Activity Center: _____

Sharing Books: _____

Guest Author: _____

TODAY'S SCHEDULE

8:30	Go to gym for assignments
8:45	Red — storyteller; yellow — activity center; green — guest author; blue — share books
9:45 – 10:00	Break — stay with your group
10:00 – 11:00	Red — share books; yellow — guest author; green — storyteller; blue — activity center
11:00 – 12:00	Red — guest author; yellow — storyteller; green — share books; blue — storyteller
12:00 – 1:00	Lunch Break
1:00 – 2:00	Red — activity center; yellow — share books; green — activity center; blue — guest author
2:00 – 2:30	Back to classrooms to discuss the day's events

(Sample Authors' Day Program — print on back of program cover; adapt to your planned program)

SUGGESTIONS FOR GROUP LEADERS

Be sure to keep your group together at all times. Encourage older students to "buddy-up" with younger students. You have a bag for holding supplies and books — it is best to carry it for the entire day. During your book-sharing time, you may go any place you like. You may go outdoors on the grass, to the library, or to an empty classroom. You will be provided with a bathroom pass. No student should be in the halls without one. At the 9:45–10:00 break, take your group to the restroom and for a drink. Then they can go outside for a breather. *Don't let them wander away!*

At 12:00 they return to their classroom for lunch. It is very important that you be back to your scheduled area at 1:00 sharp so your group can find you again. During time in the activity center, talk with your group about staying and working together. The buddy system works well. Tell them they will not have time for all of the activities, so they need to make some choices beforehand. Stress that there should be no running or roughhousing in the activity center. *Remember to stick to the schedule. That will be very important!*

At the end of the last session, give each child a certificate of participation found in your packet.

We hope that you have a wonderful day. We appreciate your enthusiasm and involvement. We will be glad to help you if there are any questions.

Thank you.

_____, Librarian

_____, Teacher

_____, Teacher

ENJOY!!!

(Sample Directions for Group Leaders)

GROUP LEADER GUIDELINES FOR HELPING STUDENTS SHARE BOOKS

1. Each student should have an equal amount of time to share his/her book and receive the group response. If you have ten students in your group and one hour of time, allow five to six minutes per child.

2. After a student has read his/her book, the group needs to give him/her positive feedback. Record the students' positive comments on the comment form provided. You may use the following questions if you feel the comments are becoming too general.

   a. What was your favorite part of the story and why?

   b. If you could be in or on any page in the book, which would you choose?

   c. Which character did you like best? Why?

   d. Do you have any ideas about how the author might continue the story?

   e. What did the author use to illustrate the book?

   f. What type of book is it? (fiction, nonfiction, pop-up, accordion, or shape book)

3. Don't forget that every child needs to feel involved. Ask different types of questions for each book and try to have each child respond, thus promoting an open group discussion. The response sheets are for you to record the positive comments and the names of the students commenting.

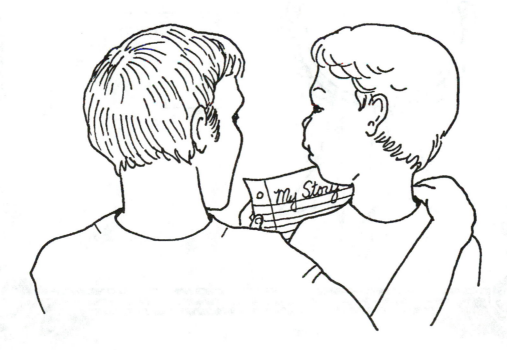

_____ **School**

AUTHOR'S CERTIFICATE

PRESENTED TO

_____

For Participating in the Student Authors' Day

_____
Librarian

_____
Principal

School Book of Academic Records

An activity that can involve the whole school and is fun for the students is a *School Book of Academic Records*. This book is patterned after *The Guinness Book of World Records* since records are kept from year to year of students' performances in various academic areas. These areas could be mathematics, spelling, geography, history, and library skills.

For example, grade one students would have a spelling bee using a list prepared by the first-grade teachers. Each first-grade classroom could send three or four representatives to take part; the remaining students will enjoy watching the spelling bee. The winner's picture (a Polaroid picture is nice since it can be seen immediately) is taken and placed on a star on a bulletin board captioned *We're Setting Records!* This record may be challenged by another student, who may then hold the record. At the end of the year the student with the best record in this category has his/her picture put in the book of records along with the level of word difficulty attained. In subsequent years there would be a winner for each year, but the record and the name of the record holder would be retained until the record is broken.

First-graders could also have a timed alphabetizing test for their library skills record and adding, subtracting, and mixed facts for their math records. Each category would have a separate page in the book with the record holder's picture, the record achieved, the best record ever achieved with that record holder's name, and the date when the record was scored.

Second-graders would also have a spelling bee from a list of words compiled by the second-grade teachers. These spelling bees would be held in the LMC with the other students watching. Number the words so that you can list the highest word level attained each year.

For library skills, they would do simple dictionary skills such as looking up a word and listing the guide words from that page. Each second grade would send two or three representatives to the library to take the timed test. The student with the fastest time and correct answers would be the record holder. In mathematics, give second-graders timed tests on addition facts to 20, subtraction facts to 20, and mixed facts to 20.

Third-graders would also do a spelling bee with a numbered word list. Their library skills would be a more difficult dictionary test, such as finding the words that would be on a page with certain guide words. This would be a timed test, and the best time for a perfect paper would be the record. In mathematics, give third-graders mixed addition and subtraction facts, and simple multiplication and division facts.

Fourth-graders would have a spelling bee with appropriate words compiled by their teachers. For library skills, try a card catalog activity, perhaps with students in teams. Each team member would be assigned a task such as finding the copyright date, locating the publisher, listing the number of pages, naming the illustrator or author, and so on from a card in the card catalog. The first team to complete their tasks correctly would be the record holder. Be sure to keep a record of their time so that it can be challenged at a later date. For mathematics, fourth-graders would do a timed test in multiplication and division and a mixed-fact test with all of the basic operations.

Add social studies to the records for the fourth grade. A good test is one involving state facts, such as the state bird, state animal, state flower, state song, state motto, and so on. It is also fun to include some questions about government officials — the name of the governor, secretary of state, the mayor of your town, U.S. senators and representatives. Naming the counties in your state from a map also makes a good timed test.

Fifth-graders are capable of handling more difficult spelling and math timed tests. Their library skills test could include a research scavenger hunt where team members (two to three people per team) hunt for the answers to questions requiring the use of reference books. Each team must use the same reference books to find the answers to the questions. This hunt should be timed, and the team with the fastest time and the most correct answers would be the record holder. Their social studies test might be identifying states using a map. They could also have a timed test in which they identify both state and capital. Another possibility might be to name the presidents in order. This too would be timed. All presidents, states, and capitals must be spelled correctly to attain a record time.

Sample record pages follow — adapt them to your own needs.

_____ **SCHOOL**

BOOK OF

ACADEMIC RECORDS

19 __ __   **19** __ __

(Sample Cover for School Book of Academic Records)

Category: _____ Grade: _____

**Place Photo
of Winner
Here**

Name: _____ Time: _____

Record Holder: _____ Year of Record: _____

(Sample Form for Record Holder Pages)

Chapter Five

STORYTIMES, BOOK TALKS, AND LIBRARY SKILLS

Although this book is not intended to be a guide for storytimes, book talks, or library skills, no media center will be successful without careful planning in these areas. The following are some ideas for each of these. To expand upon them, let your imagination and the interests of your students be your guide.

STORYTIMES

A beginning student's first contact with you and the LMC is usually in a story-time setting. If from the first session these storytimes are totally enjoyable, the student will develop a love for books and a desire to visit the library that will last a lifetime.

Storytime Rules

In order for these storytimes to be fun for you and the students, some rules must be set up from the beginning. Establish from the first visit that students must enter quietly and always sit in a designated area. Ask the teacher to accompany the class for two or three sessions to help you. Students need to learn from the start that in order to enjoy the story, they must keep their hands to themselves. An idea that works well is to have the children fold their hands and place them in their laps. You might say, "Now that you have shown me your library hands, we can begin." In each storytime the direction, "Show me your library hands," will signal the beginning of the fun.

Storytime Props

Storytimes are more fun if you begin with an activity that leads into the day's story. For instance, you could have a prop in your pocket that relates to the story and can be used for a 20-question type of game. Be sure the day's book is hidden, for students quickly catch on to the fact that the prop is related to the book. Some examples of this type of activity are a polished red pebble for *Sylvester and the Magic Pebble* by Steig; a bone for *The Amazing Bone* by the same author; a brass ring for *Big Anthony and the Magic Ring* by Tomie de Paola; a piece of spaghetti for *Strega Nona*, also by de Paola; a plastic egg for *Horton Hatches the Egg* by Dr. Seuss; or a monkey for *Curious George* by Rey (a banana for this or any other monkey story would be fun, especially if you have enough bananas for each child to receive a slice). Along this same line, a hidden apple with apple slices for all would be appropriate for Steven Kellogg's *Johnny Appleseed*.

Other pocket props could be a crocheted snowflake for snow stories, a tiny stuffed mouse for the many mouse stories, a carrot for a story about rabbits (again, a piece of the carrot for each student to eat is appropriate), a pair of glasses for *Arthur's Eyes* by Marc Brown or for *Spectacles* by Ellen Raskin, seashells for stories about the sea (one for each student is easy to acquire), a penny for a story about Abraham Lincoln, or a pumpkin seed for stories about pumpkins.

Various, easy-to-find small plastic or ceramic animals can be used for all kinds of animal stories. Plastic fruit is also appropriate for different stories. Keep your eyes open as you visit garage sales or store sales for any items relating to the stories you intend to read or tell at storytime.

Student Involvement

After reading *The Little Engine That Could* by Walter Piper, discuss with the kindergarten or first-grade students the many things that they have learned this year. Then ask if there were any things which they thought they would not be able to learn. Have each student come up and tell one thing that they have learned that they had thought they couldn't. Example: Each student starts out by saying, "I thought I couldn't learn to _____ (tie my shoes, ride a bike, and so on), but I worked at it and said 'I think I can, I think I can!' and I did it!". Then pin a little blue engine on each student. (A pattern for the little blue engine is included.)

The story *Inch by Inch* by Lionni also lends itself to an enjoyable follow-up activity: After reading the story, discuss with the students how much they have grown during the year. Ask each student to come up and be measured to see how tall they are. Write the number of inches for each child on a bright-green worm and pin the worm to the child's shirt. (A pattern for this follows.) Encourage the students to tell the story of the inchworm to their family at home.

The traditional song "The Twelve Days of Christmas" lends itself to other holidays, as well, such as Halloween. For "The Twelve Days of Halloween," you could use the following (or invent your own).

On the first day of Halloween, a scarecrow gave to me . . . a vulture in a dead tree.

On the second day of Halloween, a scarecrow gave to me . . . two smiling pumpkins.

(After each line repeat the previous gifts, as in the song "The Twelve Days of Christmas.")

On the third day of Halloween, a scarecrow gave to me . . . three costumed children.

On the fourth day of Halloween, a scarecrow gave to me . . . four howling black cats.

On the fifth day of Halloween, a scarecrow gave to me . . . five bubbling caldrons.

On the sixth day of Halloween, a scarecrow gave to me . . . six hooting owls.

On the seventh day of Halloween, a scarecrow gave to me . . . seven flying black bats.

On the eighth day of Halloween, a scarecrow gave to me . . . eight grinning ghosties.

On the ninth day of Halloween, a scarecrow gave to me . . . nine pokey pythons.

On the tenth day of Halloween, a scarecrow gave to me . . . ten munching monsters.

On the eleventh day of Halloween, a scarecrow gave to me . . . eleven dozing dragons.

On the twelfth day of Halloween, a scarecrow gave to me . . . twelve candy gumdrops.

Prepare large cards with the appropriate number of figures on it. Give a card to student volunteers. Each student stands and shows the card when his/her number is mentioned. (The patterns follow.) A candy gumdrop could be given to each child after the last card is shown.

Storytime Suggestions

When the Doorbell Rang by Pat Hutchins is a great book for storytime. Through it you can stress how much fun it is to share. Read the delightful story and have cookies on hand for everyone afterward. While the children are munching on the cookies, they can discuss ways in which they, too, can share.

Pattern books are fun for small children. Some of the many available are *A House is a House for Me* by Hoberman, *Quick as a Cricket* by Audrey Wood, *The Gunnywolf* by Delaney, *King Bidgood's in the Bathtub* by Wood, *Rain Drop Splash* by Tresselt, *Rain Makes Applesauce* by Scheer, *Someday* by Zolotow, *Crocodile Beat* by Jorgenson, *Sheep in a Jeep* by Shaw, and *We're Going on a Bear Hunt* by Rosen. These books involve students as they mimic the pattern or invent patterns of their own.

Pop-up and lift-the-flap books provide great introductory activities. Most of them are too short for the main storytime book, but children love them and will ask for them over and over again. Some good ones are by Jan Piankowski — *Halloween, Robot, Gossip* (play the game of "gossip" after this), and *Little Monster*. The "Spot" books by Hill are delightful for preschoolers and kindergarteners. There are many other pop-up books — watch for those that will enhance your storytimes. Most of these books will not withstand normal circulation, so plan to keep them on your own special shelf. At times you may wish to let students look at them as a special privilege.

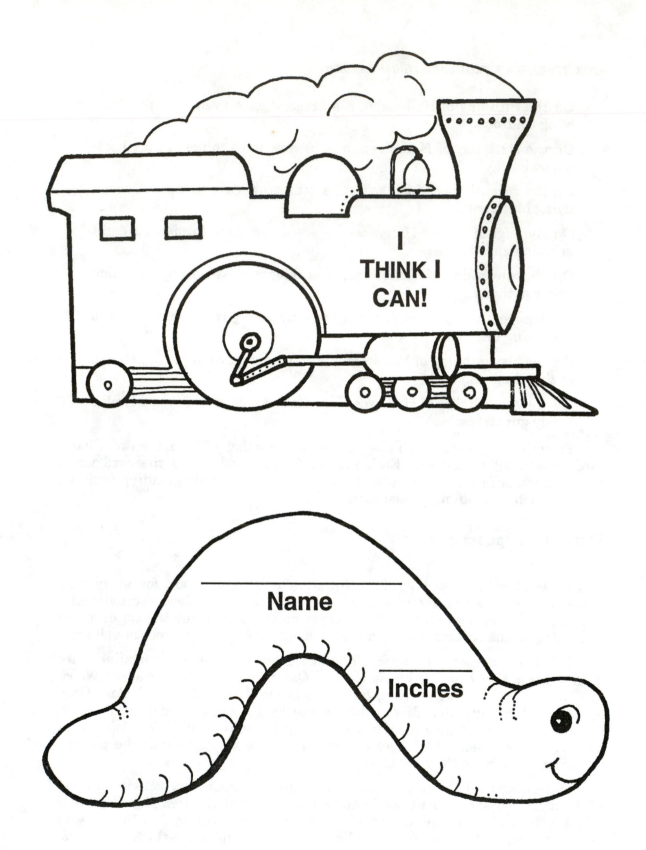

I
THINK I
CAN!

_____
Name

_____
Inches

(Patterns for *The Little Engine That Could* and *Inch by Inch*)

(Patterns for *"The Twelve Days of Halloween"* Cards — enlarge and copy the number needed for each)

(More patterns for "The Twelve Days of Halloween")

(More patterns for "*The Twelve Days of Halloween*")

Both traditional as well as modern folk tales and fairy tales provide interesting storytimes for children from grades two through five. Traditional folk tales are part of our cultural heritage and need to be preserved. The modern folk tales offer an opportunity for students to analyze and compare them to traditional tales. *The Talking Eggs* by San Souci and *Mufaro's Beautiful Daughters* by Steptoe are ideal to contrast and compare to a Cinderella story. *Lon Po Po* by Young can be compared to the traditional *Little Red Riding Hood* or *The Wolf and the Seven Little Kids*. *Sleeping Ugly* by Jane Yolen can be compared to one of the many versions of *Sleeping Beauty*. Most modern and retold folk tales and fairy tales are also beautifully illustrated and offer many opportunities to feature illustrators.

A book all children will enjoy and you will not want to miss is *The Jolly Postman* and *The Jolly Christmas Postman* by Janet and Alan Ahlberg. Since all ages enjoy this book, it is a good one to use for a school-wide activity. Have students write their own letters or make their own Christmas card to a nursery rhyme or fairy tale character. They could also pretend to be a character from one of these traditional tales and do the activity from the character's point of view.

Some author/illustrators who are especially outstanding in the field of folk/fairy tales are Vera Aardema (African folk tales), Paul Galdone (traditional tales), James Marshall (modern retelling of traditional tales), Eric Kimmel (both modern and traditional), Paul Goble (Indian legends), Tomie de Paola (Italian and Indian legends), Janet Stevens (traditional), and Demi (Chinese legends).

Chris Van Alsburg is an author/illustrator whose fantasy books are especially good for storytimes for older students. *The Polar Express, The Wreck of the Zephyr, Jumanji, The Garden of Abduhl Gazazi, The Stranger, Two Bad Ants, Ben's Dream, The Wretched Stone, The Mysteries of Harris Burdick,* and *The Widow's Broom* are all books that these students enjoy hearing and that lend themselves to interesting and lively discussions. *The Mysteries of Harris Burdick* is an excellent book for stimulating creative writing. If you don't have time for this in your classes, recommend it to classroom teachers.

BOOK TALKS

Although book talks are appropriate for younger students when you are trying to interest them in a particular type of book, you will probably use a book talk more often with older students.

Just as with the storytimes, props are useful for introducing a book talk. Hide the prop in your pocket or have a mystery box with the prop inside and let the students use a 20–questions format to guess what it is. Some appropriate props are a small plastic Indian for *The Indian in the Cupboard* by Banks or *Sign of the Beaver* by Speare, a key for *In the Keep of Time* by Anderson, a tiny doll for *The Dollhouse Murders* by Wright, a computer disk for *Space De-*

mons by Rubenstein or for *The Computer Nut* by Betsy Byars, a beetle for *Beetles Lightly Toasted* by Naylor, a worm for *How to Eat Fried Worms* by Rockwell, a spaceship for *Trouble on Janus* by Slote, a toy hatchet for *Hatchet* by Paulsen, or a star for *Number the Stars* by Lowry.

Sometimes food can be a welcome introduction, such as a batch of Turkish Delight for *The Lion, The Witch, and the Wardrobe* by C. S. Lewis. The recipe that follows is not always available in new cookbooks.

Turkish Delight

Combine and let stand for at least 5 minutes: 1/3 cup lemon or lime juice, 3 tablespoons cold water, grated rind of one lemon, and 2 tablespoons of gelatin.

In a large, heavy pan over moderate heat, put 2/3 cup of water and 2 cups of sugar. Stir until sugar dissolves. Cover pot and boil 2 to 3 minutes. Uncover and cook to a soft-ball stage, 234°F. without stirring.

Remove pot from heat and add the gelatin mixture. Return to heat and stir until candy thermometer says 224°F. Add food coloring if desired.

Pour mixture into lightly oiled 8" x 8" pan in which you have sprinkled one cup chopped nuts. Let stand for 12 hours. Sprinkle with powdered sugar and cut with buttered or sugared knife into small pieces. Pieces can also be dipped in chocolate.

Book talks can be focused on various genres, such as fantasy, historical fiction, realistic fiction, mystery, humor, biography, and so on. Give a book talk on two or three books representing the genre and have many others of the same type displayed for checkout on a nearby table.

More specific themes can also be used as a starting point for book talks; for example, survival. You could feature books such as *Hatchet* and *Journey of the Frog* by Paulsen, *My Side of the Mountain* by George, and *The Sign of the Beaver* by Speare. World War II is a theme that is interesting to both boys and girls. Some books on this theme are *The Diary of Anne Frank, The Upstairs Room* by Reiss, *The Summer of My German Soldier* by Greene, *Number the Stars* by Lowry, and *Devil's Arithmetic* by Yolen. Other themes could be school, family, friendship, sports, space travel, the future, the Revolutionary War, the Civil War, explorers, how-to-books, knights and chivalry, poetry (Jack Prelutsky can be as popular as Shel Silverstein if students are exposed to his books), and far-away places.

Check your PBS guide for possible television book talk programs that would be suitable for your grade levels.

When planning book talks, you will have to read some of the many books in your collection. You will find many of these books enjoyable and will be better able to communicate your knowledge of them to students. If you use your imagination and have fun, the students will find your talks delightful and be turned on to books!

LIBRARY SKILLS

Media specialists at the elementary-school level have the privilege and the responsibility of instilling in their students a love of learning that can be so satisfying with the acquisition of good research skills. In the elementary grades, students have their first exposure to reference sources and research. If they find the experience to be stimulating and rewarding, they will continue to develop and use these skills throughout their lives.

Suggestions for Library Skills Plans

There are many ways to teach these research skills, and all of us can use means that are creative and fun as well. There are many books available with specific plans for teaching library skills. Here are some general suggestions to help with your planning for skills.

HOW TO TEACH RESEARCH SKILLS

- Plan for lessons that are of appropriate length for that grade level
- Use "hands-on" activities whenever possible
- Try to coordinate your lessons with classroom learning
- Use new technology when available and appropriate
- Intersperse written work with more active tasks
- Use games for culminating or review lessons
- Try to use lessons that appeal to your students
- Give clear and understandable directions
- Use cooperative learning (team approach) whenever possible
- Plan for practice and review throughout the year
- Make use of community resources when appropriate and available
- Take a once-a-year trip to public or college libraries
- Vary class times by occasional storytimes or book talks
- Have fun!

When planning lessons for the various grade levels, keep in mind that an activity sheet of twelve questions may be suitable for fifth-graders but six to eight questions might be more appropriate for fourth-graders. The same applies to activities not requiring written work. Adjust your activities to the time available. If students must check out books during the same time slot as their skills classes, be sure you leave enough time for browsing and book selection.

"Hands-On" and Written Activities

Although it may seem easier to pass out an activity sheet to cover a specific skill, try to use a hands-on activity whenever possible. For example: a worksheet asking students to identify cards with author, title, or subject categories is far less effective than having the students actually use the card catalog to locate an author, a title, and a subject card. Similarly, an activity sheet in which students determine the alphabetical order of books is not as interesting or meaningful as having the students actually shelve or locate books on the shelf.

An early-in-the-year "hands-on" skills activity featuring location skills could be one using a bulletin board title, *WHO'S HERE? WHAT'S HERE? AND HOW TO FIND IT!* Post pictures of yourself and any aides and/or volunteers who assist you. Put names of each under the pictures, and list some of their tasks. Cut out pictures (or take snapshots) of encyclopedias, dictionaries, fiction books, nonfiction books, checkout desk, listening centers, computers, and so on and put them around a large map of your center.

Students can use the map to answer questions that require locating specific things in the LMC. At the end of the chapter is a sample activity sheet — or you may develop your own. This activity is a type of scavenger hunt, which can be used throughout the year for other types of research activities.

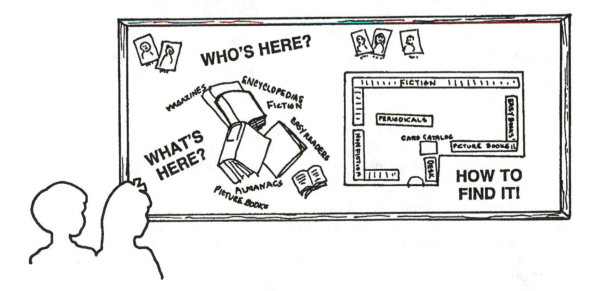

Another "hands-on" activity is to have students use cards with call numbers and titles on them to locate books. Holidays are a good time to let students pull books for you as well as get the experience of locating books. At Halloween, Christmas, Valentine's Day, and other holidays, prepare 3 inch x 5 inch cards cut from colorful cardboard. Write the holiday titles and call numbers on the cards. Add a colorful sticker representative of the holiday. Students enjoy finding the books on the shelf and will often ask to do more than you have given them.

An appropriate written activity might be one that is used for practice in the use of the almanac or dictionary. Be sure the research is either of interest to the students or an activity that is fun. Two examples of these activities are included at the end of the chapter. As students complete their written exercises, let them begin browsing for books. Staying in their seats while others finish would be a waste of time for them.

The Curriculum Connection

If you have flexible scheduling, you will be conferring often with teachers to be sure that the students are getting the library time and skills instruction they need. But even if you have fixed scheduling, talking with the teachers about areas of curriculum that they are pursuing is helpful. (See Chapter 1 for forms that can be sent to teachers requesting curriculum needs.) For example: if a fifth-grade class is studying the United States, it is a great time for you to teach the use of the almanac with its many different sections of state information. (This applies to classes studying Mexico, Canada, or other countries also.) If a class is studying the 1776 Revolution, why not compile some quotes by the famous men of that era, such as Benjamin Franklin, Thomas Jefferson, and Thomas Paine and teach the class how to use a book of quotations. If you prefer that the activity be a more volunteer one, plan a bulletin board titled *Great Quotes* and put pictures of these famous people on the board with their quotes somewhere else on the bulletin board. Students are to match the names with the famous quotations. This is also a good time to emphasize biographies, since most libraries have enough biographies of Revolutionary figures so that all the students can find one.

Classes studying the United States could receive skills instruction in using periodicals, by learning about such magazines as *Cobblestones*. Classes learning about any country might use other magazines, such as *Faces* or *National Geographic*. This also provides you with the opportunity to teach students how to use an index.

If you have computer programs that emphasize geography, such as *Where in the World is Carmen Santiago*, these can be used and enjoyed. Computerized encyclopedias can be used, whenever appropriate, to look up information in any curriculum area being taught in the classroom.

Students will appreciate finding information that they can use in their classroom, and it gives you an opportunity to teach meaningful skills. Remember to intersperse enjoyable book talks, storytimes, or skills games with your more structured skills instruction in order to provide a varied and interesting program.

Let's Find It!

Use the map of the LMC to locate the sections where you will find answers to the following questions:

1. In the reference section find an atlas. Write the name of the atlas here.

    _____

2. In the reference section locate a *World Book Encyclopedia* set. What are the letters on the spine of Volume 10? _____

3. In the reference section find the *World Almanac.* Locate the Quick Reference Index in the back of the almanac. What is the first subject listed in this index?

    _____

4. Locate the dictionaries. Locate the word *library* and write the guide words from the page where this word is located.

    _____

5. Find any book in the *E* section. Write the title and author of the book below.

    Author: _____ Title. _____

6. Find the card catalog. Find the title and call number of a book about friendship.

    Call number: _____ Title: _____

7. Find the fiction section and write the title of a book by Barbara Parks.

    _____

    Name:_____Grade:_____

(Sample Activity Sheet for Bulletin Board "Who's Here? What's Here? And How to Find It!)

It Happened in January!

Name:_____

Grade:_____

1. On which day of the week did the new year begin (January 1) in the year 1900?

   _____

2. Many college football games are played on January 1. Who won the Orange Bowl on January 1, 1979?

   _____

3. Who won the Cotton Bowl on January 1, 1975?

   _____

4. No territory ever became a state on January 1, but one did become a state on January 2, 1788. Which state was it?

   _____

5. Several presidents were born in January. Which president was born on January 30, 1882?

   _____

6. Professional football's Superbowl is played in January. In what year was the first Superbowl ever played?

   _____

Good job!

You'll soon be an almanac expert!

(Activity Sheet for Practice in Use of the Almanac)

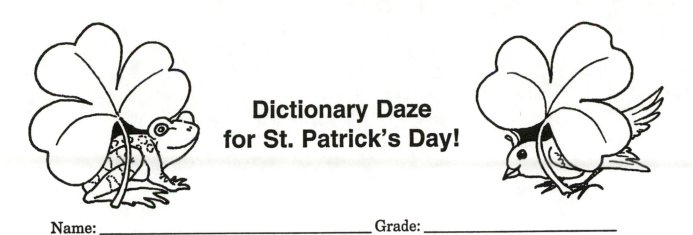

Dictionary Daze
for St. Patrick's Day!

Name: _____ Grade: _____

Look up the underlined word to find out what kind of a leprechaun to draw. Write the guide words from the dictionary page on the lines in the box.

_____ _____	_____ _____
Draw a <u>hoary</u> leprechaun here.	Draw a <u>gaunt</u> leprechaun here.
_____ _____	_____ _____
Draw a leprechaun wearing a <u>turban.</u>	Draw a leprechaun standing by a tall <u>pillar</u>.

If you have time, draw a dancing leprechaun on the back of this page.

(Activity Sheet for Use of the Dictionary)

Chapter Six

BUILDING SUPPORT WITH THE FACULTY, ADMINISTRATION, PARENTS, AND COMMUNITY

Building support for you and your programs among the faculty, your administrator, and the community is an important part of any librarian's job. Good relations between you and your administrator, you and the faculty, and you and the community can ensure the success of any planned programs, whereas poor relations with these groups can destroy even the best-planned programs. Any program you plan needs the support of the administrator, the classroom teachers, and the parents to be really successful. Following are some ideas you might use to build good relations.

BUILDING SUPPORT WITH YOUR FACULTY

Be available and helpful in aiding teachers to find books and audiovisual software that they might need for their classroom programs. Let them know that you want to provide them with all the materials they need to make their programs successful ones. Whether you supply the books from a long list of books that they want within a week or an immediate request for something they can read aloud to a waiting class, do your best to provide what they need.

One way to be helpful to teachers is to provide them with a calendar of the school months early in September. Encourage them to write into the spaces the curriculum areas that they plan to teach during each month so that you might have the materials suitable for each area. When these forms are returned to you, check your available resources to be sure you can supply the needed materials. Since this calendar is merely an overview and not to be considered as a definite request, also provide each teacher with a form they can use for their immediate specific requests. (See sample.)

To keep track of materials requested and the date when the materials are needed, it is helpful to have a schedule posted above your desk. A calendar with writing space within each date could be used. On the date when requested material is needed, write the name of the teacher and the material requested.

Be an Available, Willing Resource

Another way to be an available resource to teachers is to have bibliographies ready for them on a variety of topics. You will often be asked for lists of books on many different topics, and you can be prepared by saving prepared bibliographies that you find in professional magazines. On each bibliography, put a check mark beside each title that is in your library and then save the bibliography in a file. When you prepare a special bibliography for an individual teacher, make a copy of it for your own file. With a computerized library system, a bibliography can be quickly prepared. If you keep an extra copy for your files, you will save time by having the material immediately available for the teacher.

Name: _____ Grade: _____

Curriculum Areas to Be Covered During the _____ School Year

MONTHS	LANGUAGE ARTS	SOCIAL STUDIES	HEALTH/SCIENCE	OTHER
September				
October				
November				
December				
January				
February				
March				
April				
May				
June				

Return to the LMC when completed. Thank you.

(School Calendar)

© 1993 by The Center for Applied Research in Education

_____ School Media Center

Request for Materials

I need: (put check marks by needed materials)

_____ Books

_____ Audiovisual Materials

On the following topics:

_____

_____

_____

I need these materials by _____.

I will need these materials in my classroom for _____ weeks.

Teacher: _____ Grade: _____

(Request Form for Materials)

From Your LMC:

Please write below any requests you might have for books or audiovisual materials that you would like to see purchased for the LMC. We will try to purchase as many of them as possible.

Title	Author	Publisher	Price
_____	_____	_____	_____
_____	_____	_____	_____
_____	_____	_____	_____
_____	_____	_____	_____
_____	_____	_____	_____

Use the back of this page if necessary.

(If you do not know specific titles, indicate subject area.)

Please return to the LMC. Thank you.

_____
(Librarian)

Name: _____ Grade: _____

(Request Form for New Books and AV Materials)

Many teachers will request books they have seen or heard about in workshops. Often, you will find that these books are out of print and no longer available from jobbers or book stores. In this case, look for the requested books in bookstores that sell used books or try to purchase a book with a similar theme for the teacher.

When materials you have ordered for a specific teacher arrive, check them out to him/her and send the materials with a brief note such as the following:

Hurray! We found it!

Here is the _____ that you requested we buy for the LMC.

It has been checked out to you first so that you may enjoy it.

_____, Librarian

Bad News and Good News!

We were unable to find the _____
that you requested, titled _____,
because it is no longer available. However,
we purchased this _____,
titled _____, as a possible
substitute.

It has been checked out to you first so you can see if it fits your needs.

_____, Librarian

(Response Notes for Requests)

Other Ideas for Being an Available Teacher Resource

_____

_____

_____

_____

_____

_____

_____

_____

_____

_____

_____

Be Fair

Always try to be scrupulously fair in providing materials to your faculty. The distribution of available audiovisual equipment is often a headache since teachers are sometimes convinced that another grade level always gets the best television/VCR combination or the best motion picture projector. You can avoid the suspicion of favoritism with the following method. In the spring when materials are turned in to you for maintenance or repair, request that teachers fill out an audiovisual request form by grade level. (A sample form is included here.) Then in the fall before school begins, have the requested material set out together with a sign specifying the grade level. Through this method you can share the best equipment because you can rotate each piece rather than allowing a first come, first served method. If the fifth-grade classes had the best movie projector in the previous year, assign it to another grade level. Make sure each grade level gets some of the best equipment. For example: if the grade level has asked for four cassette players, try to give them one or two of your best players and then complete the order with some that aren't as good. When the equipment is checked out to an individual classroom, each grade level can decide among themselves who gets which piece of equipment. When necessary, they can share the best equipment.

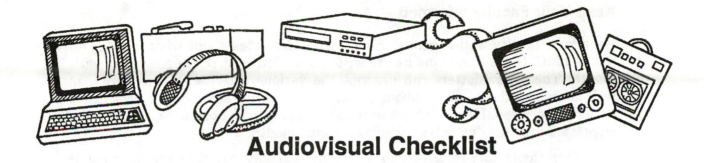

Audiovisual Checklist

Teacher: _____

Grade: _____

Please mark each item with the number that you would like for your grade level.

Overheads: _____	Record Players: _____
Tape Recorders: _____	Tape Players: _____
Filmstrip Projectors: _____	Filmstrip Viewers: _____
Movie Projectors: _____	Televisions: _____
Filmloop Projectors: _____	VCRs: _____
Language Masters: _____	Earphones: _____
Jack Boxes: _____	Computers: _____

(Opaque projectors and slide projectors will be checked out from the LMC when needed.)

(Form for Audiovisual Checklist — Add or Delete Items to Fit Your LMC)

Keep Your Faculty Informed

Keep your faculty well-informed. Send them brief notes about what is going on in the LMC. Some librarians like to write a newsletter at the beginning of each month. These newsletters can describe the various activities in the LMC, as well as inform the teachers about any new equipment, software, or books that may have arrived. Head each letter with an appropriate book stamp, or use the suggested drawings we have included for each month.

Keep the faculty informed about audiovisual software that you have available that they may not be aware of. Often, there are pieces of software in the storage closet that were purchased several years ago and have been forgotten by the faculty. Before withdrawing these materials, give the teachers the opportunity for one last look at what is available. Some of it may be just what a teacher needs for a teaching unit. Invite the teachers to the LMC for an Audiovisual "Tea." A good time for this tea might be during conference times or during an in-service day. Use the forms included for your "tea."

For this tea have your audiovisual software displayed by curriculum area. Let the teachers browse among the materials to see what they can use. Have video players, filmstrip projectors, and other pieces of equipment on hand so that the teachers can try out the software. It is a great deal of work to pull all of the software, display it, and then return it to its proper place, but it may be worth it if materials are again in use. Provide the teachers with forms on which they can list items that they'd like to use along with the date that they anticipate such use. These turned-in forms could be used for a drawing for a door prize sometime during the day. Serve tea, coffee, or soft drinks along with a plate of cookies.

Be an Active Participant

It is often difficult to feel that you are a part of a close-knit staff because you are often unable to be in the faculty room when other staff members are there. At recess time when teachers often have a break, you are usually busy in the LMC with the students who have come with free-time passes to spend their recess. Since you can't visit with teachers at this time, try to plan your lunchtimes so that you can sometimes eat with primary-grade teachers and at other times with upper-grade teachers so you can get to know them and what is going on in your school. If possible, try to visit occasionally with teachers before or after school. This may be difficult because of the many demands on your time, but it is definitely worthwhile.

Be Aware and Concerned

As you work with various teachers, try to recognize each teacher's individual style and needs. When you see something in a magazine or professional journal that fits his/her particular interests or curriculum needs, you can make a copy of the article and put it in the teacher's box or, better yet, take the time to personally deliver it. Following are some other suggestions that will help you demonstrate your interest in each teacher.

SEPTEMBER NOTES
FROM YOUR LMC

OCTOBER
NOTES
FROM YOUR LMC

NOVEMBER NOTES
FROM YOUR LMC

(Sample Headings for LMC Newletters)

DECEMBER NOTES FROM YOUR LMC

JANUARY NOTES FROM YOUR LMC

FEBRUARY NOTES FROM YOUR LMC

(Sample Headings for LMC Newletters)

MARCH NOTES
FROM YOUR LMC

APRIL NOTES
FROM YOUR LMC

MAY NOTES
FROM YOUR LMC

JUNE NOTES
FROM YOUR LMC

(Sample Headings for LMC Newletters)

Please come to the LMC

on _____ from _____
to _____ o'clock. Come when
you can, and stay as long as you can to
browse through our new and used
audiovisual items. Come and see what
you can use while you enjoy treats as
well as have the chance to win the
door prize.

_____, Librarian

- -

Welcome to your LMC!

Please write down the titles of any
items you think you would like to use
in the coming year.

If you can, please give us an approximate
time when you will need the item.

Title: _____ Date needed: _____

Title: _____ Date needed: _____

(Please use the back of this form if you need more room.)

Return this form to the LMC. We will try to fill all of your requests as stated.

_____, Librarian

Name: _____ Grade: _____

(LMC Invitation to Browse and Welcome to Your LMC — Request Form)

During National Book Week (or National Library Week), as a special treat, attractively gift-wrap for each teacher a new uncirculated book that you think the teacher will enjoy. Attach the following poem (or one similar) to it:

Here's a book that's fresh and new

We've checked it out just for you!

Happy National Children's Book Week!

Another idea suitable for either National Children's Book Week or for National Library Week is to put a large button advertising reading or books (purchased through library supply catalogs) in each teacher's mailbox. Leave a note with the button asking the teacher to wear the button during the special week to advertise books and reading. Mention that the button is a gift for them from the LMC.

By these and other small gestures during the year, you can show your concern for them and their programs, and your desire to help.

Other Ideas for Gaining Faculty Support:

_____

_____

_____

BUILDING SUPPORT WITH YOUR ADMINISTRATOR

Your administrator can be your greatest ally in advancing your programs for the LMC or he/she can be the biggest block to achieving them, so it is of prime importance to build a good relationship with your administrator.

Some of the ways you can do this are

1. Keep your administrator informed of the LMC activities.

2. Keep your administrator aware of the circulation figures.

3. Be professional in your appearance and in your behavior.

Keep Your Administrator Informed

Keeping your administrator informed and knowledgeable about your media center programs and needs is of primary importance. Make an appointment to discuss upcoming programs with your administrator. Be sure that he/she receives all notices, notes, and letters that are sent to either faculty or parents. Send invitations to your administrator for events that are occurring in the LMC, such as an author visit, a book club celebration, a visiting storyteller, or an interesting exhibit. Be sure to discuss library/media center needs during the year and explain how your requests can make the LMC program a better one.

The circulation figures will indicate to the administrator how much the LMC is being used. It is simple to call up these figures if you have a computerized system. It is more time consuming if your system is not yet computerized. Counting the number of items checked out each day takes time, but it could be worthwhile to gain support for the LMC. Perhaps a student aide could count the cards for you, or it could be part of the daily duties of your aide or a parent volunteer. Submit the numbers to your administrator at the end of each month so that he/she can see the multiple number of items that are checked out from the LMC.

Be Professional In Working With Your Administrator

You want to be a friend to your administrator and have him/her be a friend to you, but you also need to maintain a professional attitude at all times. Dress in a neat, attractive manner. This does not mean that you cannot don a costume on special days, but it does mean that clothes worn on the weekend for leisure activities are probably not appropriate for the LMC.

Even more important than how you dress is maintaining a professional attitude. It is important that your administrator knows that you need more aide time or a larger budget, but present these issues in a logical, well-planned way, rather than complaining about how understaffed or overworked you are. If your administrator wants you to take on one more duty or job and you feel that it will interfere with your primary duties, don't be afraid to present your reasons for your reluctance to tackle one more task — but do it in a professional manner. Writing down your schedule and what you do at each time slot and then showing this to your administrator may help him/her see the inadvisability of assigning the additional task to you.

Your administrator wants the LMC to be an attractive, well-run addition to the school and will be willing to work with you to achieve this if you have built a positive relationship with him/her.

BUILDING GOOD RELATIONS WITH PARENTS AND THE COMMUNITY

Some ways you can build positive feelings among parents and the community for your library/media programs are as follows:

1. Keep them informed.

2. Solicit their participation in LMC activities.

3. Provide them with useful information.

4. Allow them to check out material (for a sick child, for preschool children, for a college class, for a scout troop, and so on.

BUILDING GOOD RELATIONS WITH YOUR CUSTODIAN

Your custodian can be your best friend in achieving a successful LMC program. He/she will not only keep your facility clean, he/she also repairs shelves, moves heavy equipment, and carries boxes of new materials to and from the office. The custodian needs to be aware of any special programs you are planning for your LMC. The following two forms may be of use.

_____ (Date)

Dear _____,

On _____ we are planning a special program in the LMC.

We will need your help in the following ways:

Thank you.

_____, Librarian

Dear _____,

Thank you for your help with our special program in the LMC on _____.

We really appreciate it.

_____, Librarian

("Please Help" Form and Thank You Note)

Keeping Them Informed

Students who enjoy using the LMC and are excited about the programs are the best advertisement for you and your programs. Short articles by you about the exciting reading promotions and other activities can be regularly printed in your school's newsletter. When an author or an illustrator visits, be sure you describe it, too, in the newsletter. Call your local paper and explain that an author is visiting and ask if they would be interested in sending a reporter to cover it. During National Children's Book Week or National Library Week, send an article to the local paper about some of the things that are taking place in your LMC.

A sample article could be something like this:

Students at _____ Elementary School will be celebrating National Children's Book Week by coming to school on Wednesday morning, November ___, dressed as their favorite book character. At two o'clock on that day all the students will gather in the auditorium and have a favorite book character parade.

This activity is sponsored by the school's Library/Media Center.

Taking pictures of students as they participate in your reading promotions and other activities is another way to keep parents informed. These pictures can be posted on a hall bulletin board near the LMC so that parents can look at them when they are in the school building.

Being pleasant and helpful in explaining procedures or programs is, of course, always important. Before beginning a reading promotion, especially one for children in the primary grades, be sure to send a note home to parents explaining the program and what children need to do to participate.

In the fall, it is a good idea to send a note home to parents after the first visit of children in kindergarten and first grade. The note can tell the parents about the day of the week when their child is scheduled for the LMC, the number of books that can be checked out, the length of time these books may be used, some ideas on book care, and tips on how to encourage their child to read. A sample letter is included. Adapt it to your own program or write a letter of your own.

Letters encouraging parents to help their children learn the love of reading are appropriate to send during National Children's Book Week, National Library Week, or just before summer vacation. Two sample letters are included here.

Communicate with parents often. Keep letters and notes as brief and as clearly stated as possible. In all of your communications with parents (and staff and administration as well) be enthusiastic and excited about reading, books, and your LMC programs.

Dear Parents,

Today your child is bringing a book home from your school library/media center. This book may be kept for one week. Please help your child with the following things:

1. Help to develop a love of reading by enjoying the book with your child. Spend time with the television off so that you may enjoy reading together.

2. Remind your child to have clean hands when reading books, to use a bookmark, and to turn the page from the upper right-hand corner.

3. Help your child find a good, well-lighted place to read.

4. Remind your child to return books on time.

5. Send damaged books to school for repair. Please do not mend library books at home.

6. Help your child to find a place for his/her library book which is out of reach of pets or little brothers or sisters.

7. Give your child a plastic bag in which to carry his/her book when returning it in bad weather.

_____ is your child's library day. Help your child to remember to bring the book back to school on or before that day.

Thank you.

_____, Librarian

_____, School Library

(Dear Parents Letter)

HELPING CHILDREN BECOME BETTER READERS

© 1993 by The Center for Applied Research in Education

We all want our children not only to be good readers, but also to know the joy of reading. One of the first things you can do to ensure your son's or daughter's love of reading is to read to your child. Begin as soon as possible and continue as the child grows older. By reading to children, they can absorb the beauty and flow of language without thinking about the mechanics of reading.

As our children become good readers, we are often tempted to push them or urge them to read books that are within their reading abilities but that are above their understanding. It is not enough that children can read the words, they must also have had enough of life's experiences to understand what the author is trying to say. If they read a book before they can understand it, they will have lost that book forever, since they probably will never read it again at a time when they can understand it.

Don't be alarmed if your child brings home a book that you feel is too "easy" for him/her. Some researchers think children read in wavelike patterns—at times reading easy books, then harder books, and then back to easy ones again. Reading books that are easy for them is not only enjoyable, but it helps them gain speed in reading. A child reading an easy book that he/she enjoys is learning a love of reading, and we need not be concerned that they will stop their reading development at that stage. One day they will become bored with their easy reading and will move on to another author or another type of book.

Probably the most important thing we can do to foster reading, other than by reading to our children, is to let them see us reading for enjoyment and knowledge. Try to set aside a time during the day or evening when the TV set is off and the whole family reads for half an hour or an hour. Right before bedtime is a good time, for it seems a privilege to children because it may delay their bedtime. It also puts them in a happy, restful mood for sleep.

During this National Children's Book Week, why not try a no-TV time and substitute reading time instead. The children will benefit from it, and the entire family will enjoy it.

_____, School Librarian

(Helping Children Become Better Readers)

SUMMER IS HERE!
A PERFECT TIME TO READ!

Summer will soon be here, and your children will be asking, "What can I do?"

Be ready for that question with some ideas for summer reading. Check with the public library to see what summer reading programs they are sponsoring. Be willing to take your children to the library to participate in the reading programs and storytimes.

Show your children that reading is important to you as you take time to sit down and enjoy a good book. Relax in the shade of a tree and read a good book to your child. Turn off the tired reruns on television and see what a pleasant time can be enjoyed by the entire family as they read or play games.

Sit down with your older students and help them make a list of books that they would like to read during the summer. Your school or public librarian can help with lists of books that are appropriate for your child.

Enjoy the summer, and *don't forget to read!*

_____, School Librarian

Solicit Their Involvement

Parents and members of the community who help in the LMC or in any of its programs are probably going to be enthusiastic supporters of your LMC activities. Encourage parents and community members to volunteer to work in the LMC or to volunteer their expertise in storytelling, speaking about their hobbies, demonstrating a skill, or in displaying their collections or hobbies.

Some ways in which parents can help you in the LMC are:

- Checking in returned books
- Typing requests for information
- Filing materials in the vertical file
- Helping with bulletin boards
- Shelving books
- Repairing damaged books
- Supervising small groups of children.

In September, send home a note with each child in your school giving parents the opportunity to volunteer. Let them list the things they would most enjoy doing. After they become volunteers, try to let them do this type of work in your LMC.

Often, there are members of the community who would enjoy working in your LMC. Letters to service clubs or retirement groups, such as the American Association of Retired People or American Association of Retired Teachers, might bring offers of either volunteer help or the names of people who would be willing to speak or to display hobbies or collections. Sample letters to both parents and community groups are included. Adapt these letters to your own needs.

Provide Useful Information

Be prepared to supply parents with information they will find useful. Bibliographies of suitable books are sometimes requested by parents. At other times, you may be asked to supply books or information to help parents guide their learning disabled child or to suggest books to challenge a talented or gifted child. You may also be asked for advice in finding books for parents to check out which give ideas for arts and crafts projects that could be used for scouts or similar groups. Books on other countries or states are sometimes requested by parents if they plan to take a trip there. Some of these books will be found in your collection of children's books. Your collection of crafts books or books on foreign countries or other states will have what parents need, but information to help parents with their parenting skills will not be in your children's collection. Purchasing a few of these books would be helpful to parents if your budget allows it.

Some possible titles of the many available are:

Cultural Literacy by E. D. Hirsch
The Read Aloud Handbook by Jim Trelease
Encourage Your Child to Read by Nancy Larrick

1001 Ways to Improve Your Child's Schoolwork: An A-Z Guide to Common Problems and Practical Solutions by Lawrence J. Greene

Bringing Out the Best: A Resource Guide for Parents of Young Gifted Children by Jacqulyn Saunders

Guide to Raising a Gifted Child: Recognizing and Developing Your Child's Potential by James Alvino

Other Titles to Purchase for Parent's Use:

_____

_____

_____

Some magazines that parents will appreciate and children will also enjoy are:

Challenge: Reaching and Teaching the Gifted Child published by Good Apple

Creative Kids published by GCT, Inc.

Other materials that would be helpful to parents are videos to help them with their parenting. Some possible titles are:

Gary Coleman — For Safety's Sake published by LCA

ABC's of Homework published by GM

Multiplication Rock published by Golden Book Videos

Parents involved with after-school sports for children might appreciate the availability of some teaching videos such as:

Head to Toe Soccer for Little Leaguers published by Best Film and Video Corporation

Golf for Kids of All Ages published by Brentwood Home Video

Learn How to Dance — Ballet for Kids published by Butterfly Video

To keep parents informed of the availability of these videos, they could be shown in the LMC or in the halls during open house or during conference times.

To keep parents informed of summer opportunities for their children, you could prepare a list of workshops or other activities available for children during these months. The workshops or activities might be sponsored by the city parks and recreation department, a science museum, or a nearby university or junior college. City libraries usually provide summer reading programs and you could receive information about these programs from the public librarians. Print the list of summer opportunities for the educational advancement of children in your school paper or send home this information to parents with your end-of-the-year letter.

By keeping parents and community informed, by encouraging their participation, and by providing them with useful information, you will build positive feelings and support for your LMC and its many programs.

Dear Parents:

Parent volunteers are a much appreciated group in our LMC. We hope that some of you would like to volunteer to help in our LMC this year.

Some of the tasks that we ask our volunteers to do for us are repairing damaged books, putting plastic covers on paperback books, checking out books to students, checking in returned books, shelving books, preparing or taking down bulletin board displays, supervising students in the LMC during the noon hour so that the librarian can go to lunch, and typing letters to various companies requesting materials for the vertical file.

In addition to the above, we also appreciate it very much when parent volunteers share their talents or hobbies. If you are a good storyteller, we would love to have you tell stories to small groups of students. If you have a collection or a hobby that you could talk about or display, please let us know. Some of you may have taken trips to interesting places and would be willing to share your experiences with the students.

Please indicate your interests on the form below and return it to the _____ LMC.

Thank you.

_____, School Librarian

© 1993 by The Center for Applied Research in Education

Please check any that apply. Thank you.

_____ I would be willing to volunteer to help in the LMC. I could work from _____ to _____ o'clock on _____ of every week.

I would especially enjoy doing _____.

_____ I would like to share my talents as a _____storyteller.

_____ I have a collection I could share. (Please explain: _____.)

_____ I would like to demonstrate a craft or hobby. (Please explain: _____.)

_____ Other (Please explain: _____.)

Your name: _____ Phone number: _____

(Sample Volunteer Letter to Parents)

Dear President of _____:

In our library/media center at _____ School, we often have guest speakers and loaned exhibits. We also have volunteers who help in our LMC in many capacities. As a civic organization, we know of your past and present interest in education and in our children. We would like you to share with your members our invitation to participate in the educational process by being a volunteer in our LMC or by sharing your hobbies, interests, or talents.

If any of your members would like to volunteer to work in our LMC, we would welcome them. If any of them are especially knowlegeable in a field that would be of interest to children, we would like to invite them to volunteer to speak to a group of students in our media center. If any of your members have a special hobby or collection that they would be willing to share by exhibiting it or explaining it to the children, it would be much appreciated.

Please share our invitation to participate with your membership. Thank you for your help. Please contact me at _____ School (phone: _____) for more information or to offer to share your talents with us.

Sincerely,

_____, School Librarian

_____ Library/Media Center

(Sample Volunteer Letter to Civic Groups — Type on school letterhead stationery)

Chapter Seven

BUDGETING FOR SUCCESS

Whether you have a very small budget or a very large one, careful planning is essential to make the best use of your funds.

Some things to consider are

1. Taking stock of your present budget and planning with your supervisors

2. Thinking of other possible funding sources

3. Making careful use of funds

TAKING STOCK OF YOUR PRESENT BUDGET AND PLANNING WITH YOUR SUPERVISORS

Planning for next year's budget usually is done in the spring of the preceding year. Before meeting with your principal to make any final decisions on a budget, take careful stock of this year's funds and your present allocations. Most LMCs allocate funds in categories similar to this: books, audiovisual software, equipment, periodicals, supplies, repairs, and special programs. Look carefully at each allocation and its amount. Were your book funds depleted early in the year while audiovisual software funds were more than sufficient? Were your repair and supply funds adequate or were they gone before the middle of the year? You may wish to study your allocations and see if the funds can be better distributed.

When you have decided what percentages of your budget each fund should be allocated, determine with your principal the amount of your entire budget. Some districts have central control of all the LMCs in the district. In this case, the amount of your budget is usually based on the number of students in your school. In other districts, the principal has sole control over his/her school's budget. In yet others, the school is under site-based management, in which a group composed of the principal, some teachers, and one or two parents works out the budget for the school. In the first instance, you will probably have little control over the amount you receive, but in the latter two instances, be ready with figures to present to either the principal or to the site-based management team. If there has been a price increase in books, software, or equipment, be ready with examples. When enrollment increases, explain how this presents a need for additional money, especially in supplies. Sometimes a change in curriculum means increased funds, such as when the whole language and literature-based curriculum became popular and put a greater demand on trade books from the LMC. Do not be afraid to state your case clearly. An excellent LMC program benefits the entire school, and both teachers and the administration want you to have the resources you need if at all possible.

When you meet with your principal, supervisor, or site-based committee, have your facts and figures in a well-organized written form. Have enough copies of this written form so that your principal/supervisor or members of the site-based committee can have the information to look at as you present your budget. Leave these copies behind to enable them to further study these facts and figures at a later time.

The following is a form for you to use in planning and presenting your budget for the coming year.

PROPOSED BUDGET FOR

_____ SCHOOL

FOR THE _____ SCHOOL YEAR

Proposed total budget: _____

Last year's total budget: _____

BUDGET #	CATEGORY	LAST YEAR	PROPOSED
_____	Books	_____	_____
_____	Periodicals	_____	_____
_____	AV Software	_____	_____
_____	Computer Software	_____	_____
_____	Supplies	_____	_____
_____	Equipment	_____	_____
_____	Repair/Maintenance	_____	_____

© 1993 by The Center for Applied Research in Education

Rationale for any changes: _____

_____

_____

_____

_____

_____

_____

_____

(Proposed Budget Plan)

OTHER SOURCES FOR FUNDING

Book Fairs

Aside from the general school budget, there are other sources for funding which you might consider.

An annual or semiannual book fair is both profitable for the LMC and fun for the students. There are many commercial suppliers of book fairs, such as:

GREAT AMERICAN BOOK FAIRS
2827-A 29th Ave.
P.O. Box 7649
Olympia, WA 98507

TROLL BOOK FAIRS
100 Corporate Drive
Mahwah, NJ 07430

SCHOOL BOOK FAIRS
401 East Wilson Bridge Rd.
Worthington, OH 43085-9970

WALDEN BOOK FAIRS
P.O. Box 10016
Stamford, CT 06913-0160

Book fairs can also be arranged with local bookstores or nearby jobbers. There are advantages and disadvantages to each. With commercial book fairs, the books are delivered in cases which need only to be opened for display and sales. Sample letters to parents are provided along with book lists for children. Promotion posters and flyers are also often supplied. Professional book fair companies require no inventory and provide easy record keeping. Your commissions are usually in both books and cash. The disadvantage to commercial book fairs is that you are not able to choose books for your students but must take whatever the company supplies.

With local bookstores or jobbers, the advantage is that you choose the books you want for your fair and also the number you wish for each title. Dealing with local businesses is also good for public relations. The disadvantages are that you must pick up the books, set up your own displays, return any unsold books, and often keep a more exact inventory. Percentages are usually in cash and are not as good as they are with commercial book fairs. No promotional items are included, and you need to prepare your own letters to parents, posters and flyers, and book lists for student use before the fair.

Parent-Teacher Organizations

Parent-teacher organizations can be another source of funds for the LMC. They are sometimes willing to give money for purchasing special items such as encyclopedias or sets of reference books. They also are often willing to provide funds for your reading incentive programs. Many parent-teacher organizations have a set amount that they give to the school's LMC every year for these special programs.

Donations and Service Organizations

At times books are donated to your library, and they are often an asset to your collection. Books are sometimes donated in memory of someone or to honor a retiring teacher or staff member. If the donor wishes you to purchase the book, be sure to choose a book that is beautiful (Caldecott medal winners are appropriate), well-made, and of lasting interest. A bookplate naming the honored person, the year, and the donor should be placed in the front of the book. It is a good idea to check the book out first to the donor.

Service Clubs are another possible source of additions to your budget. They will sometimes supply the funds for the purchase of special kinds of books, such as a set of science books or sets of books of state or local interest.

Used-Book Sale

If your school district policy and your supervisor approve, a used-book sale is another source of income. As you withdraw books from your inventory throughout the year, set them aside for your book sale. Remove call numbers, cards, card pockets, and bar codes. Cross out any identifying school names, and stamp "Withdrawn" somewhere at the front and back of the book. Let teachers see whether any of the books can be used in their classrooms, and then sell the remainder of the books at a sale near the end of the school year. Price the books very reasonably so that all students will be able to afford a book if they desire. A letter to parents explaining why the books are being sold would be good public relations. A sample letter follows.

_____ (Date)

Dear Parents:

On _____ (date), there will be a sale of used books from our LMC. These are books that have been withdrawn from our collection because they are too worn for continued circulation. Although no longer suitable for multiple checkouts, they are still usable and would provide good reading for your children.

Other books to be sold are books that are damaged, but might be useful for their beautiful illustrations which could be cut out and used for reports, room decoration, or creative-writing activities.

Books are priced reasonably, with many selling for a quarter or fifty cents, which will make it possible for most students to purchase a book.

Funds from this book sale will be used to purchase new books for our LMC.

Sincerely,

_____, Librarian

(Sample Letter to Parents Explaining Why Books Are Being Sold — Type letter on school letterhead)

Grants

Grants are another possible source of funding. Your district may have funds available for grants or your state may be a source of grant money. There are also federal grants available. It is advisable to investigate the possibility of grants from private enterprises, too.

Once you have identified grant sources, study each of them to determine what type of requests are most frequently approved. Determine how you would use the requested grant money. When writing your grant, you will need to be very specific — indefinite or vague requests will not be successful. Before writing your grant you should discuss it with your principal or supervisor. If you are unfamiliar with writing grants, check with grant-writing manuals or contact people who have written grants and ask for their advice.

All this is certainly time-consuming, but it may be worthwhile since you will be able to fund programs that otherwise would be unaffordable.

MAKING CAREFUL USE OF FUNDS

Since money is always in short supply, it is important to use your funds wisely. Be sure you purchase books and other materials that will be used by both students and staff. Some suggestions that may be helpful follow.

1. Read reviews in professional journals and keep a card file on items you wish to purchase.

2. Add to your card file recommended titles from teachers and students.

3. Add titles that fill out subject areas that have been depleted or need updating.

4. Visit jobbers or book supply stores that offer schools a good discount (10 – 20 percent is customary). Be sure to take your list of

previously reviewed and desired titles. It is always helpful to see the books if possible, since some books, even with the best reviews, may be physically unattractive or not appropriate for your school's population. Another advantage is that you will see many good books that you might not otherwise discover.

5. Consult with other librarians in elementary-school libraries. They will usually be able to recommend many good titles. It is helpful when going book buying to go with one or two of these librarians, for you can help each other in selecting titles.

6. Plan to share materials to avoid duplication of expensive titles in districts large enough for more than one elementary school. Also, with whole language reading programs many teachers want several copies of one title. Rather than purchasing six or seven copies yourself, borrow from other schools and be willing to share your books in return.

7. Investigate the possibility of borrowing materials from your city, local college, regional, and state libraries. They may have titles that you may need on a rare occasion but do not wish to purchase for your own collection. At times, parents may be willing to share a particular book that is needed and not in your collection.

8. Don't forget to look carefully through discount catalogs. Some offer books with library bindings and excellent reviews at substantially reduced prices. Most of the books offered have recent copyright dates.

A sample form to use in your "wish list" card file is below.

Cards can be removed from your "wish list" card file after materials have been received.

Keeping track of your funds is always important. A form that you may use and keep in a three-ring binder follows: Fill in budget title and budget numbers for each category. Record purchases and balance remaining. Don't forget shipping and handling charges when ordering from catalogs.

Author:_____

Title:_____

Publisher: _____

Copyright date: _____ Price: _____

Reviewed in or recommended by:

_____

_____ School LMC

Budget for _____ School Year

Category: _____

Budget Number: _____   Allotted Amount: _____

DATE	AMOUNT SPENT	REMAINING BALANCE

(Budget Form)

Chapter Eight

SELECTION POLICIES, CENSORSHIP AND COPYRIGHT

Written policies approved by the district for the selection of materials, censorship, and copyright give the media specialist/librarian a sense of security. With these policies, the media specialist has a basis from which to operate. She/he knows the reason for the material selections, knows what can be done if materials are challenged, and is secure in knowing what can or cannot be copied.

If your district does not have these policies, it is important that you work with your staff and administrators to draw them up. If your district does have policies in place, be sure you are familiar with them. Policies that are several years old may need revision and updating. When you find it necessary to formulate a selection policy or revise an old policy, a committee made up of all the media specialists/librarians from the district, a media supervisor, and a curriculum director should be formed.

SELECTION POLICIES

The selection of materials should be a cooperative, continuing process involving administrators, teachers, media specialists, and students. The basic factors influencing selection are the curriculum; the reading interests, abilities, and backgrounds of the students using the libraries; and the amount of available funds. The media specialist of each school is primarily responsible for selecting the materials, and as such must be sure that his/her choices are in agreement with the philosophy statement that emphasizes your district's beliefs of what constitutes appropriate materials for their students.

After making your philosophy statement, outline your goals for the selection of materials. Some possible goals could be to provide:

- Materials that will help students make intelligent choices in their everyday life.

- Multicultural materials reflecting our many ethnic and religious groups.

- Materials expressing both sides of controversial issues.

- Nonsexist, unprejudiced materials.

- Materials that promote accepted values, an appreciation of beauty, and an appreciation of literature.
- Materials that complement and enhance the curriculum.
- Materials that are appropriate in content and in reading level for the student population.
- Quality materials using accepted review sources to aid in your selection.

After a selection policy is written, it will have to be approved by your local school board. After approval, copies of the policy should be sent to all school libraries, school offices, and district offices.

Be familiar with your selection policy because it will give you confidence in your selections and justification for your choices should anyone question them.

CENSORSHIP

It is possible that at some time someone may question the suitability of a particular book or other material in your LMC. When this happens, you may be understandably upset. No one likes to have their choices questioned. However, if you realize that the material is being challenged and not you, perhaps it will help you to deal with the situation. Often you may not even be aware that there is anything questionable in the material being challenged. No librarian is able to read all the books or view all the audiovisual materials before they are placed on the shelf, and even though reviews in professional journals are helpful, they also can be misleading. Listen to the complainant with courtesy and understanding. Make no admission of guilt or any commitment to remove the material. Often a simple discussion with the challenging parent is enough to handle the complaint. If the parent is not satisfied with your explanations, however, you need to have a procedure to follow in handling the challenge. It is of the utmost importance that your school or district have a censorship policy in place to handle such challenges. School districts should not be bullied into removing books or other material. Each challenge must be handled carefully before any decision is made.

After you have spoken personally with the complainant, it is helpful for you or your principal to acknowledge in writing that you have received the complaint. A sample letter is included. If the complainant is not satisfied with the written response, most districts would require the complainant to fill out a form that states what the material is and why he/she objects to it. (A sample form is included here.) This completed form should be presented to the district

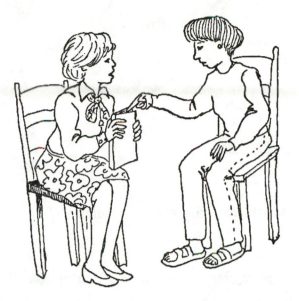

superintendent, who will read the complaint and send copies of it to the principal and media specialist of the school involved. The superintendent should then call together a committee for review of the challenged material. This committee should be composed of the building administrator, teacher in the subject area of the questioned material, the curriculum director, a parent representative, the media specialist from the school whose material is challenged, and possibly a layperson interested in schools. The members of this committee should carefully study the completed form, and then the person or group making the challenge should have the opportunity to present his/her views to this committee in person. After hearing the complainant, the committee should then study the challenged material as objectively as possible. The members of the committee should read reviews of the material as well as the material itself. They should take into consideration the importance of freedom to learn and to read. The challenged material must be read or viewed in its entirety, rather than taking the challenged section out of context.

After the committee has made a decision as to whether to retain the material or to have it removed, the findings should be presented to the school board for action. Copies of the committee's report and the subsequent action of the board should be sent to all schools in the district and to the complainant.

Occasionally, the complainant and the school district may work out a compromise regarding the challenged material. For instance, the material may be judged to be suitable for older children and be sent on to the media center in a middle school or high school.

When faced with a challenge, do not take it personally. If you feel strongly that the challenged material is worthwhile, be ready to defend it, remembering the inherent right of freedom of choice and the right to read. Be understanding, however, of a parent's concern for his/her child's moral and ethical development, and attempt to be as helpful as possible in reaching an agreement.

_____ (Date)

Dear _____ :

Thank you for your concern over the appropriateness of _____ in our Library Media Center.

Our school district has a policy for the selection of materials. We are sending you a copy of these policies to help you understand the selection process. If you still have concerns about the material in question, please complete the enclosed Citizen's Request for Reevaluation of Materials form and return it to me.

I can assure you that this matter will be given our prompt attention. If the form is not returned within two weeks, we will assume that you no longer wish to file a formal complaint.

Thank you again for your concern about our media center selections. We appreciate your interest in our school and in our students.

Sincerely,

_____, Librarian

© 1993 by The Center for Applied Research in Education

(Sample Letter to Complainant — copy on school letterhead)

Name of person requesting reevaluation: _____

Address: _____

Telephone: _____

Complainant represents: _____

    _____ (himself or herself)

    _____ (an organization) Name of organization: _____

Type of material protested:

    _____ Book Author: _____

                Title: _____

                Publisher: _____ Copyright date: _____

    _____ Audiovisual materials:

                Type: _____

                Title: _____

                Producer: _____

    _____ Other materials, please specify: _____

What do you object to in this material? (Please list specific paragraphs, pages, chapters, and so on.)

_____

_____

_____

_____

Why do you feel this material is objectionable?

_____

_____

Would this material be appropriate for another age group? _____

What age group would be appropriate? _____

Have you read, seen, or heard the material in its entirety? _____

(Sample Citizen's Request Form for Reevaluation of Materials)

Do you find anything of value in the material? _____ If so, what? _____

_____

_____

In your opinion, what is the main idea of this material? _____

_____

_____

_____

Have you discussed the material with your school librarian or media specialist? _____

In your opinion, what action should be taken by the school in regard to this matter?

_____

_____

_____

Do you have any recommendations of other materials that could replace this item if it were to be removed from the school's media center? _____ If so, what? _____

_____

_____

_____
(Signature of Complainant)

(Sample Citizen's Request Form for Reevaluation of Materials — continued)

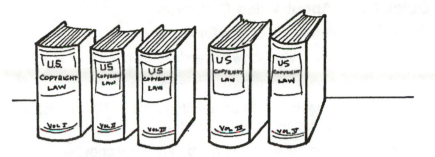

COPYRIGHT

As a media specialist, you will probably be your school's authority on copyright laws. If your district has a copyright policy, become familiar with it *before* you are asked to copy something. If your district does not have a copyright policy, it would be wise to develop one in cooperation with the other media specialists, building principals, and the superintendent.

If you need further assistance and guidelines, write for the Librarian's Copyright Kit, Order Dept., American Library Association, 50 East Huron Street, Chicago, Illinois 60611. There is a charge for the kit. Another place where information may be obtained is AEME (Association for Education Media and Equipment), P.O. Box 865, Elkader, Iowa 52043. There is also a hot line for copyright questions. The number is 1-800-444-4203.

When you have determined your school's copyright philosophy, be sure that you, yourself, are very familiar with fair use guidelines for off-air-taping and photocopying. Be careful that you always obtain permission before you copy any copyrighted works. Always follow copyright laws so that you set an example for both staff and students. Be sure you communicate the district's copyright philosophy to the teachers in your school. Schedule time during a faculty meeting when you can explain the copyright rules to the staff. Hand out a printed copy of the copyright policies of your district to each staff member. Emphasize the importance of following copyright procedures. Take time to stress the policy with regard to video and computer program copying, for this is where many problems arise. Explain that you will not be able to copy written, video, or sound material that is covered under copyright. Ask that teachers be responsible for teaching students what a copyright is and the ethical as well as the legal reasons for not abusing copyright laws.

Post a simple sign above the copy machine where all can see it. (A sample sign follows.) A sign posted somewhere on each VCR and computer would also be advisable. Since the librarian/media specialist is sometimes also held responsible for copyright infringement, having a signed statement that you have posted copyright laws may be prudent. Keep a copy of this statement and ask the principal to keep the original. (A sample statement follows.)

Quick Facts About Video Copyright

When using rented videotapes for classroom use:

1. Videos must be shown in a classroom or other space used for teaching.

2. Videos must be shown in a face-to-face setting to students and educators.

3. Videos used should be an integral part of the educational program as outlined in teacher lesson plans.

4. The video shown must not be an illegal copy.

Guidelines to Video Off-Air Recording

1. Schools may record off-air broadcasts and retain them for a period no longer than 45 days after the recording.

2. After 45 days, all off-air recordings must be erased or destroyed.

3. Off-air recordings may be shown once to a classroom and then repeated once for reinforcement if necessary.

4. Off-air recordings must be made at the specific request of a teacher or teachers and not made in advance in anticipation of requests.

5. Portions of the off-air recording may be used, but the recording may not be altered or electronically merged with other recordings.

6. Off-air recordings must include the copyright notice of the original broadcast program.

Copyright Notice Form

This is to record the fact that on _____ (date), the statements of copyright/copying procedures were posted near the copy machine, on the VCRs, and on the computers in _____ School.

_____, Librarian

_____, Principal

BE AWARE OF

COPYRIGHT LAWS

BEFORE USING THIS MACHINE!

(Copyright Notice Sign — to be posted above machines)

Chapter Nine

KEEPING UP WITH NEW MATERIALS AND SURVIVING TECHNOLOGY

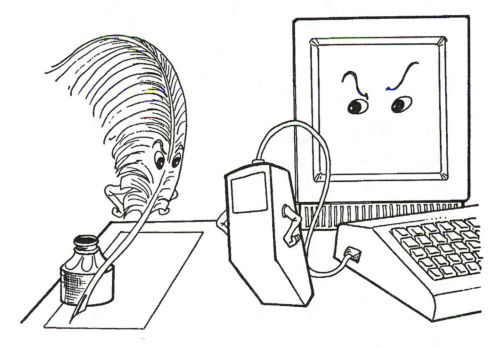

With most elementary school librarians teaching classes 50 to 90 percent of the school day, how can the time be found to keep up with new materials and ever-changing technology? Following are some suggestions to help you keep up with both new materials and new technology

KEEPING UP WITH NEW MATERIALS

Since it is important to have your collection as up to date as possible, time must be set aside for examining professional reviews of materials; looking at publishers' catalogs; discussing materials with other librarians, teachers, and students; and browsing through bookstores for new arrivals. Although browsing through bookstores must wait for weekends or after-school hours, don't feel guilty about setting aside a block of time during each school week for material selection. With the flood of new materials readily available and the constraints of ever-shrinking budgets, great care must be taken to ensure that you will select materials that fit your school's needs.

Professional Journals

Professional journals will probably be your most-often-used source for keeping up with what is new in books and media. These professional journals are expensive, so if you have several elementary schools in your district, each school could subscribe to a different publication and then share with one another. If you are the only elementary school, try to examine these publications and then choose one or two titles that best fit your needs.

Some excellent publications that contain reviews of books and media are *School Library Journal, The Horn Book, Booklist, Library Talk, Bulletin of the Center for Children's Books, Instructor* Magazine, *Teacher, Learning, The Reading Teacher,* and *The Web.*

When looking at reviews and publishers' catalogs, keep in mind the curriculum needs of your various grade levels. In order to be informed of their needs, try to attend the grade-level meetings or planning sessions of the various grades. Informal talks with the teachers can also make you aware of their needs.

As you go through the professional reviews in publications, keep wanted titles on index cards (example of card in Chapter 6) and file alphabetically by author. These cards will speed up your ordering process and ensure that you will not miss wanted titles. Keep these cards as an ongoing file throughout the school year, adding to the file whenever you see titles that you want for your LMC.

The information you put on the card may seem to be too time-consuming, but it will reduce your ordering time. Specifying the source of the review will help you if you have forgotten the material, so be sure to include the date of the publication as well as the title of the publication. You can then refer to the source for a reminder of why you wanted this particular item. The copyright date of the book is also important, even though it need not be mentioned in your purchase order. If you have the card filed and then do not order for a long time, the book may be unavailable because many books go out of print and are not reprinted. Another important reason for including the copyright date is so you can be sure, especially in the case of nonfiction materials, that you are getting items that are as current as possible.

After looking at reviews in professional magazines and publishers' catalogs, and noting your wants on your order cards, be sure to put a check somewhere on the cover of the magazine or catalog to show that you have finished with it. Then file the catalog or magazine in a file alphabetically by title, being sure to remove any older editions.

Other Ways to Learn About New Materials

Another way to keep abreast of new materials is by attending workshops in curriculum areas and professional conferences of school media specialists. Bookstores often supply lists of new titles that can be helpful in finding needed materials.

Teachers often request titles that you can add to your want list cards. When ordering, if you find these requests are for titles no longer available in hardback, check paperback catalogs and prebound paperback sources for their availability.

Ordering Periodicals for Staff and Students

Periodicals for both staff and students can be used extensively or largely ignored, depending on your selections. From time to time, take a survey of the magazines to determine which magazines are being used and should be continued and which are no longer popular. Periodicals ordered for both staff and students can lose their popularity and should be replaced with new publications. (Survey forms for staff and students follow.)

Periodicals — What's Your Choice?

(Please list below your two favorite professional
magazines now available from our LMC.)

_____

_____

Are there any other professional magazines that you would like to see in our LMC?

Please list them below.

_____

_____

_____, Teacher

Student Periodicals Survey

What is your favorite children's magazine?

_____

_____

Are there any magazines that you would like us to order

for our LMC? Please list them below.

_____

_____

Name: _____ Grade: _____

(Periodical Survey Form for Staff and for Students)

Other ways to learn about new periodicals are through free samples which sometimes come to the LMC and through advertising found in other publications. Other librarians and parents are also good sources.

If you hear of a good magazine and would like to see a sample before ordering, you could use the following form or one like it to request one. This form can also be used (with slight modifications) when requesting other materials, such as catalogs or information for your vertical file.

Dear _____:

Please send the following for use in our elementary-school Library Media Center:

_____

_____

_____

_____

_____

This material will be used with students as a supplemental reference source in our center.

Thank you for providing this service to our school. Without such services, it would be difficult to provide our students with these beneficial materials.

Please send the materials to me at the above address. Thank you.

Sincerely,

_____, Librarian

© 1993 by The Center for Applied Research in Education

(Form for Requesting Materials — copy on school letterhead)

Ordering Times

It is probably best to plan a time for ordering so you can be sure of getting up-to-date materials. A good time to place book orders with jobbers might be in September, ensuring that books will arrive in time to be used for most of the school year, and then order again in May, for billing in your new fiscal year. This should allow the jobber to have your order filled and in your library when school starts again in September. If you have kept up your ongoing file of wanted materials throughout the year, the ordering should not be too difficult or time-consuming. Remember that ordering appropriate materials is an important part of your job, and time needs to be reserved for it.

SURVIVING TECHNOLOGY

Some media specialists/librarians are delighted and excited about the technological advances in LMCs. Others may be frightened and insecure about the changes. Computerizing the LMC is an area of concern as is the advancing technology in all forms of communications. Because it is such a vital concern to media specialists, perhaps it is best to first consider the value of computerizing your media center.

Computerization of the LMC

Computerization is expensive, and so your first consideration should be whether it will be worthwhile for your particular LMC. If you have a small school with a small collection, it may not be worth the time and money it will take to computerize. If, however, your school is large, your collection is a large one, or you are in a district where you can network with other libraries, you will probably want to computerize.

Advantages

Some of the benefits of computerizing are

- Easy, quick checkout
- Maintains circulation records
- Keeps track of items on reserve
- Easily produces overdue lists and notices
- Monitors problem patrons
- Searches are broader because of multiple key words
- Generates bibliographies from extensive key words
- Provides for faster inventory
- Prints labels
- Allows for networking with other school media centers

Disadvantages

Some of the drawbacks of a computerized system are

- Very costly
- Requires a great amount of time to install
- Requires training time
- Computer system can "go down"
- When system has problems, it takes time to restore normal operation

Before you computerize, also consider the following:

- Does your school district have a plan for coordinating the computerization of all schools in your district?
- What are your district and school needs?
- Which computer companies have programs that fit these needs?
- How will the expense of computerization be funded?
- How will the program be implemented?

District Planning

If your district has more than one school, it is important to plan together for the computerization of all the LMCs. Uniformity in your programs will mean that you can network your collection and help each other when problems arise.

A committee of some or all of the media specialists should be formed to study the needs of the district and the various programs available. The committee should visit LMCs that are computerized to get ideas and to hear the advantages and disadvantages of each program. Prepare a questionnaire to send to each company offering a library computerization program. A sample questionnaire follows. Add to it any items that you feel are important and delete any that you feel are not necessary. After the companies return the questionnaire, determine which best meet your needs. The representatives of these companies should be invited to visit with the committee and present their programs. Each program should be evaluated using criteria developed by the committee.

The questionnaire could be sent to the following companies that supply computerized systems:

WINNEBAGO SOFTWARE COMPANY
437 East South St., P.O. Box 430
Caledonia, MN 55921

NICHOLS ADVANCED TECHNOLOGIES INC.
3452 Losey Boulevard South
La Crosse, WI 54601

CASPR, INC.
20111 Stevens Creek Blvd.
Suite 270
Cupertino, CA 95014

FOLLETT SOFTWARE COMPANY
809 North Front Street
McHenry, IL 60050-5589

MEDIA FLEX, INC.
Box 1107
Champlain, NY 12919

LIBRARY AUTOMATION PRODUCTS
38 Pond Street, Suite 301
Franklin, ME 02038

UNISYS
Box 500
Blue Bell, PA 19424-0001

Name of Company: _____

Address: _____

_____

We are considering computerization of our Library Media Center. We have formed a committee which has been studying the different types of computer programs available for use in media centers/libraries.

After our research was completed, our committee formulated a list of things which we feel are important in our computerization program.

Will you please fill out the questionnaire and return it to us? Thank you.

Sincerely,

_____, Media Specialist

(Sample Letter to Send to Library Computerization Companies — Copy on school letterhead)

Please put a check beside each feature that applies to your program.

_____ 1. Provides integration between circulation and catalog

_____ 2. Provides for direct input of complete MARC records and accepts these records from a secondary source

_____ 3. Able to store complete MARC records

_____ 4. Menu-driven system

_____ 5. Uses industry-standard barcodes

_____ 6. Prints barcodes

_____ 7. Supports barwand and/or scan stand

_____ 8. Circulation supports a portable barwand reader for inventory, check in and out, and creating lists

_____ 9. Password control for all systems

_____ 10. Catalog allows for simple author/title/subject searches

_____ 11. Catalog allows for Boolean search using and/or/and not

_____ 12. Allows searching by key words from MARC fields

_____ 13. Supports truncated searching

_____ 14. Generate bibliographies

_____ 15. Circulation system tracks books to specific patron

_____ 16. Circulation system determines status of books (in or out)

_____ 17. System is able to switch from one patron to another quickly

_____ 18. Provides patron access to circulation status

_____ 19. Provides complete overdue functions and reports

(Sample Questionnaire to Send to Library Computerization Companies)

© 1993 by The Center for Applied Research in Education

_____ 20. Allows user to customize reports

_____ 21. Provides choice of formats for output — screen, printer, disk

_____ 22. Touch screen capability

_____ 23. Accepts batch mode of data entry, deletion, and editing

_____ 24. Password required for check out to patrons with overdue materials

_____ 25. Calculates fines when applicable

_____ 26. Provides for speedy inventory

_____ 27. Capable of networking

_____ 28. Provides on-line help messages

_____ 29. Company provides retrospective conversion of records to MARC format

_____ 30. Company provides on-site training

Cost?_____

_____ 31. Company provides toll-free telephone support

Cost?_____

Computer required for your program? _____

Complete cost of this program? _____

Additional comments: _____

_____

_____

_____

_____   _____
(Signature)   (Title or Position)

(Sample Questionnaire to Send to Library Computerization Companies, continued)

After reviewing the returned questionnaires, visiting various computerized schools, and talking with representatives of companies supplying systems, determine the program you feel is best suited to your particular needs. Be sure the program fits in with the district plans as determined by your technology committee. Remember that the software for the system is more important than the hardware, so select your automation program first and then purchase the necessary hardware to run it.

Throughout the planning for your system, make sure you have the support of your principal, since it is easier to get the funding if your administration is behind you. If the district cannot fund the program, try to get a grant or gift from a local business, or perhaps your parent-teacher organization can make it their funding priority for the year.

Whenever possible, plan to have retrospective conversion of your collection done by the company supplying the system. This is expensive but well worth the cost to get your book collection on line. If your district feels this is too expensive, insist that the LMC be closed for a period of time, usually four to five weeks (depending on your collection), so that you can be trained by the company representative and then devote all your time to getting your collection on line. (This can be done during the summer if the district has the funds to pay you.) Volunteers should be obtained to help. They can put on barcodes, and some may even be skillful at entering information in the computer. Sometimes local high school or college students who are computer literate can be hired at a reasonable wage.

Before putting on barcodes and doing any entering, weed your collection extensively. You do not want to spend time entering items that will soon be withdrawn. When entering your collection, it is advisable to purchase a system that will pull up the MARC records for thousands of books. You can then enter these records and add local cataloging data. Most books will be found in these systems, and the few that aren't will have to be entered individually. The company supplying the automation program will be able to recommend or sell you one of these programs. They are a nominal price when you consider the time saved and the more complete MARC records you will access. Once you have your present collection in the system, new acquisitions can also be found on these programs, and yearly updates are available. When ordering, remember that many publishing companies provide disks with MARC records which can then be loaded into your system.

After your collection is entered, you will then have to enter the names, addresses, room numbers, and so on of the student patrons and staff. Students may be provided with a card with their name and barcode, or you can keep a folder for each classroom with the names and barcodes of the students. Students usually learn their barcode number quickly, but until then you can scan it from either the card or the class folder.

When getting your system up and running, feel free to call the toll-free number of your support system. If questions are not of immediate concern, keep a notepad and jot down any concern for later consultation.

If you need to close the LMC to start up your system, try to be as helpful as possible with your staff and students. It is probably not advisable to let students check out materials, but allowing the staff to check out a room collection will help them get through the time period when the LMC is closed. (This should probably be at the end of the school year or at the beginning.) If the barcodes are on the books, the code numbers can be written in a notebook under the teacher's name. When the system is in place, you can then check them out with the computer using the barcode numbers. When the system is finally functioning, the staff and students will soon forget the earlier inconvenience and be enthusiastic about the benefits of the computerized system.

Other Technology Concerns

The variety of new technology can be overwhelming to even the most technology-minded specialist. New software and/or hardware seem to appear on the market daily. The librarian/media specialist feels that there is neither the time to learn the new technology nor the funds to purchase them.

To keep from becoming totally frustrated with advancing technology, the media specialist needs to realize that it will be impossible to purchase all that is available. Working with a schoolwide or district committee involving building principals, teachers, and media specialists, guidelines can be developed to determine the direction your district wants to pursue.

Such guidelines will be a big help to you as you try to determine how your funds should be spent, and they will provide some justification if teachers or staff question your allocation of funds. Be sure teachers are kept informed of decisions you or a technology committee have made. For example, some of you may have already decided that films will soon be almost completely replaced with video disks, so you have not bought the new projectors some teachers are requesting. If these teachers are part of the overall plan or are at least made aware of why you do not replace the projector, they will be more cooperative and adaptable. Similarly, if you have decided to purchase a computerized encyclopedia for a CD ROM, they need to know that this is the reason you have not purchased the new encyclopedia set that they think is needed.

The following charts might be useful as you plan your technology needs and purchases. You will probably be the one responsible for getting information to teachers and staff about the various equipment and software, so you will need to know what is currently available. After you or your technology committee have filled out the charts (or similar ones of your own devising), hold an informational meeting so that you can inform the staff about the many options. Then let them help decide which equipment and which software is of the greatest need.

Once again, keep in mind that even though the abundance of materials can be confusing, you will be able to choose what will be most useful to your school and students if you take the time to study the available options and consult with your technology committee members and your staff.

AVAILABLE TECHNOLOGY — EQUIPMENT

ITEM	USES	COST	# NEEDED	RECOMMENDED BY

AVAILABLE TECHNOLOGY — SOFTWARE

ITEM	USES	COST	# NEEDED	RECOMMENDED BY

Chapter Ten

INVENTORY AND WEEDING

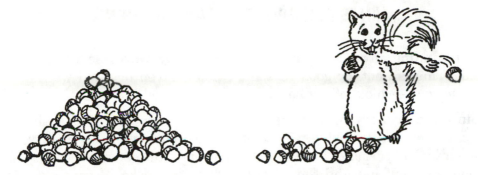

Inventory and weeding are two of the librarian/media specialist's tasks which are time-consuming and likely to be neglected unless a period of time is set aside for doing them. Although these tasks are not as exciting as many of the other activities in the LMC, they are important in order to maintain an interesting, useful, and current collection.

Both inventory and weeding can be conducted as an ongoing activity throughout the year, but time also should be planned for a more complete inventory/weeding at the end of the school year. If you have an extended contract, this creates no problem. If you do not have this time, try to arrange with your principal for an early closing during which time you will be able to complete your inventory/weeding tasks.

Some administrators may not understand the importance of having the time provided for inventory/weeding, so you must be ready with the reasons to justify a request for early closing. Here are some reasons for you to consider.

- In order for the card catalog to be useful to staff and students, it must be accurate, up-to-date, and compatible with the materials in the collection. (You may have to explain what this means to your administrator.) If your library is computerized, you will still need to remove titles from the computer if you find that they are missing for the same reasons you remove them from your card catalog.

- While taking inventory, you can spot books that are cataloged incorrectly or shelved incorrectly.

- Books needing repair can be removed for that purpose.

- Out-of-date, inaccurate, or biased books can be found during inventory and removed from the collection.

- Subject area needs may be found at this time. (Nonfiction interests vary greatly from year to year, and certain areas may need to be expanded.)

- Removing books that have not been checked out for many years provides space on the shelves for new acquisitions.

- There is a monetary responsibility to the community to monitor the collection.

- Other points pertinent to your particular LMC:_____

_____

_____

HINTS FOR INVENTORY AND WEEDING

Before beginning inventory, try to have as many books as possible already shelved. (This is another good reason for doing inventory and weeding at the end of the year — most of the books have been turned in.)

Since the primary purpose of inventory is to compare your shelf list with your collection, you probably will want to have your shelf list with you when you inventory. If possible, have an assistant or volunteer with you so that one can read the shelf list and the other can find the books. Because you are the one responsible for the weeding, it is best for you to find and examine the books while your assistant reads the shelf cards. In the case of a computerized library, the books are inventoried by using the barcode scanner. Some librarians put the barcodes on the spine of the book so that the book can be inventoried without removing it from the shelf. Others put the barcodes inside the front or back cover. This has the advantage of requiring the person doing the inventory to remove the book from the shelf to determine whether the book should be retained or withdrawn from the collection. Some of the reasons for withdrawing a book are

- Worn, torn, or dirty condition
- Sexist or biased
- Out of date (particularly in nonfiction, although some fiction illustrations are so dated they do not appeal to students)
- Inaccurate information
- Poor circulation record (For example, books that have not been checked out in four or five years should probably be pulled. With a computerized system, print a usage report to find out this information.)

WEEDING GUIDELINES

FICTION: Watch for fads that have passed — such as the many fiction books that come out after the issuing of popular movies — books about *Star Wars* or *The Karate Kid* would be an example. Books that no longer have any appeal to your students can be discarded. Obviously sexist or biased books should be weeded. Books that are no longer checked out, probably due to old-fashioned illustrations, can be pulled.

PICTURE BOOKS:	As in the fiction section, care must be taken to remove obviously biased or sexist books. Books that are clearly miscataloged and should be in either the fiction or non-fiction section should be weeded at this time and recataloged and correctly shelved. Books in this section are the ones that are most likely to be damaged, so try to look inside the book for torn, dirty, or child-colored pages.
REFERENCE AND GENERAL WORKS:	Out-of-date encyclopedia sets should be pulled (these may be given to classrooms). Overused and out-of-date almanacs should be pulled (although you may wish to keep usable volumes so that you have enough for large-group instruction). Out-of-date indices, such as *Children's Guides to Magazines*, *National Geographic* Index, *Cobblestone* Index, and so on should be discarded and replaced with more current indices.
PHILOSOPHY:	Keep what is relevant to your school population. Remove books on ethics in which the text is either too difficult or the illustrations are unappealing. Carefully examine your books about the occult to be sure they are appropriate for the age group of your school.
RELIGION AND MYTHOLOGY:	Look over your books on religion to be sure you have a sampling of the many world religions. In order to make room for new books on religions, you may need to withdraw older books from a subject already well covered. There are many beautiful new books on mythology, so check carefully for old ones, especially collections. If they are not being used much, remove them to make room for newer, more appealing ones.
SOCIAL SCIENCE:	Books on government need to be checked for accuracy and readability. Books dealing with careers and occupations need to be updated every five or six years or as need arises. The holiday section needs frequent careful checking to weed out unattractive and unused books. Although folk tales and fairy tales never go out of style, the many lavishly illustrated new volumes available may justify pulling the older, less attractive, and less used books.
LANGUAGES:	Weed unused volumes to make room for more interesting books. Most dictionaries can be retained, but discard old classroom volumes.
PURE SCIENCE:	This section needs frequent careful revision because of the constant advances in science. Be especially careful in the sections on the universe, weather, and scientific experiments. Check carefully for accuracy of information and for copyright dates. The section on prehistoric animals also needs to be checked for accuracy as well as

for signs of excessive wear and tear. Books on wild animals, plants, and rocks may not go out of date as rapidly, but they need to be checked for usage, beauty, and clarity of text.

TECHNOLOGY: Rapid advances in technology require that books in this section be checked for copyright date. Five to seven years will change the information in fields such as medicine, television, planes, cars, trucks, motorcycles, space technology, robotics, and even cooking. Remove out-of-date books in these fields.

ARTS AND RECREATION: Beautifully illustrated art and music history books need no discarding, so check only for damaged or worn condition. Drawing and crafts books need more careful inspection because of their popularity. Discard worn or unattractive books to make room for new additions. When you inventory the music section, check with the music teacher on questionable volumes. Hobby books on such things as stamp or coin collections need to be replaced often because of changing monetary values. Books on movies and television quickly become outdated. Remove the outdated to make room for new volumes.

Sports books that are "how-to-play" types will not become outdated as quickly as books on professional teams. Pay special attention to sports books in regard to difficulty of text. Keep this section well weeded to accommodate new additions.

LITERATURE: The poetry and drama sections do not need much weeding, so check primarily for unused books. The jokes and riddles section needs frequent checking for damage and wear and tear.

HISTORY, GEOGRAPHY, AND BIOGRAPHY: Historical books need not be discarded unless they are inaccurate or in poor condition. Geography and travel books need to be discarded and replaced more frequently due to changes constantly taking place in today's world. Biographies of sports and entertainment personalities can be discarded when their popularity wanes. Keep collected biographies suitable for your age group. Biographies of historical characters should be retained, especially if they are being used.

At the end of the chapter are reproducible charts that you can use for your inventory. Record the number of books pulled in each section and also the areas in the section that you would like to expand. List specific titles that you have pulled and would like to replace with the same title if possible or if the title is no longer available, with a book that is a close substitute. When your inventory is completed, you can use these titles and concerns to help you as you prepare your order for the coming year.

WHAT TO DO WHEN INVENTORY IS COMPLETED

When the inventory is completed, you then need to pull cards from the card catalog for books that are missing or that have been pulled. In a computerized system, you need to remove these titles from the computer. Your administrator might like to have a printout or a typewritten report of the number of books currently missing and the number of books weeded from the collection. Computers will generate these reports for you. If you do not have a computer, it will not take long to type a brief report, especially if you have kept the charts and listed the number of books pulled in each section. Missing books are not usually considered missing until they have been gone from the shelf for at least two years. When working with a shelf list, you can note the year when the book is first discovered to be missing; for example: "Missing — 1993." Put a paper clip at the top of the card to designate it as a missing book. This will be an indicator to help you determine how long the book has been gone. In the event the book is returned, remove the paper clip and erase the "Missing —" notation. If your library is computerized, check your system's manual to see how to handle missing books.

MAKING PROVISIONS FOR WITHDRAWN BOOKS

You will probably have several hundred weeded books on your hands when your inventory is completed. What to do with these books is sometimes a problem. If your district permits, you can have a used book sale. (See Chapter 7 on budgeting.) If you don't wish to do this or your district will not allow it, see if there are other schools in the area that could use the books. Check with the classroom teachers and see if some of the titles could be used in their classrooms. In some districts, the books are boxed and the custodian in each school takes them to the warehouse. Whatever you decide to do, be sure each book is clearly marked "Discarded" and all identifying marks of your school crossed out or erased.

Inventory and weeding are time-consuming and at times difficult, but when completed, your LMC will be more efficient and workable.

INVENTORY AND WEEDING CHART — FICTION

SECTION	NUMBER PULLED	BOOKS, AUTHORS, OR SUBJECTS (replacements or additions)
Fiction A–D		
Fiction E–I		
Fiction J–N		

(A Form to Use for Inventory and Weeding — keep track of number pulled
and titles you wish to reorder, or substitute titles to replace pulled items)

SECTION	NUMBER PULLED	BOOKS, AUTHORS, OR SUBJECTS (replacements or additions)
Fiction O–S		
Fiction T–Z		

Special notes on fiction needs:

(Inventory and Weeding Chart — Fiction, continued)

INVENTORY AND WEEDING CHART — EASY SECTION

SECTION	NUMBER PULLED	BOOKS, AUTHORS, OR SUBJECTS (replacements or additions)
Easy (Picture Books) **A–D**		
Easy (Picture Books) **E–I**		
Easy (Picture Books) **J–N**		

**(A Form to Use for Inventory and Weeding — keep track of number pulled
and titles you wish to reorder, or substitute titles to replace pulled items)**

SECTION	NUMBER PULLED	BOOKS, AUTHORS, OR SUBJECTS (replacements or additions)
Easy (Picture Books) **O–S**		
Easy (Picture Books) **T–Z**		

Special notes on needs in the easy section:

(Inventory and Weeding Chart — Easy, continued)

INVENTORY AND WEEDING CHART — NONFICTION

SECTION	NUMBER PULLED	BOOKS, AUTHORS, OR SUBJECTS (replacements or additions)
Reference		
Philosophy		
Religion/ Mythology		

(A Form to Use for Inventory and Weeding — keep track of number pulled
and titles you wish to reorder, or substitute titles to replace pulled items)

SECTION	NUMBER PULLED	BOOKS, AUTHORS, OR SUBJECTS (replacements or additions)
Social Science/ Government		
Social Science/ Careers		
Social Science/ Transportation		
Social Science/ Holidays		
Social Science/ Folk Tales/ Fairy Tales		

(Inventory and Weeding Chart — Nonfiction, continued)

SECTION	NUMBER PULLED	BOOKS, AUTHORS, OR SUBJECTS (replacements or additions)
Languages		
Pure Science/ Experiments		
Pure Science/ Universe		
Pure Science/ Rocks/ Minerals		

(Inventory and Weeding Chart — Nonfiction, continued)

SECTION	NUMBER PULLED	BOOKS, AUTHORS, OR SUBJECTS (replacements or additions)
Pure Science/ Prehistoric Animals		
Pure Science/ Trees and Plants		
Pure Science/ Wild Animals		

(Inventory and Weeding Chart — Nonfiction, continued)

SECTION	NUMBER PULLED	BOOKS, AUTHORS, OR SUBJECTS (replacements or additions)
Technology/ Invention and Medicine		
Technology/ Trains, Planes, Cars, Trucks, and Motorcycles		
Technology/ Space Travel and Robotics		
Technology/ Fashion and Cooking		

(Inventory and Weeding Chart — Nonfiction, continued)

SECTION	NUMBER PULLED	BOOKS, AUTHORS, OR SUBJECTS (replacements or additions)
Technology/ Pets		
Arts and Recreation/ Fine Arts		
Arts and Recreation/ Drawing		
Arts and Recreation/ Crafts		
Arts and Recreation/ Music		

(Inventory and Weeding Chart — Nonfiction, continued)

SECTION	NUMBER PULLED	BOOKS, AUTHORS, OR SUBJECTS (replacements or additions)
Arts and Recreation/ Movies and Television		
Arts and Recreation/ Hobbies		
Arts and Recreation/ Games and Sports		

(Inventory and Weeding Chart — Nonfiction, continued)

SECTION	NUMBER PULLED	BOOKS, AUTHORS, OR SUBJECTS (replacements or additions)
Literature/ Poetry		
Literature/ Drama		
Literature/ Jokes and Riddles		
Literature/ Story Collections		

(Inventory and Weeding Chart — Nonfiction, continued)

SECTION	NUMBER PULLED	BOOKS, AUTHORS, OR SUBJECTS (replacements or additions)
History/ Exploration		
History/ Flags, Names Heraldry		
History/ Wars		
History/ Foreign Countries on Other Continents		

(Inventory and Weeding Chart — Nonfiction, continued)

SECTION	NUMBER PULLED	BOOKS, AUTHORS, OR SUBJECTS (replacements or additions)
History/ Native Americans		
History/ United States		
History/ North America (Canada, Mexico, and Central America)		

(Inventory and Weeding Chart — Nonfiction, continued)

SECTION	NUMBER PULLED	BOOKS, AUTHORS, OR SUBJECTS (replacements or additions)
History/ South America		
History/ Travel		
History/ Biographies		

Special notes on needs in the nonfiction sections:

(Inventory and Weeding Chart — Nonfiction, continued)

Chapter Eleven

AVOIDING BURNOUT: Enjoying Your Job to the Fullest

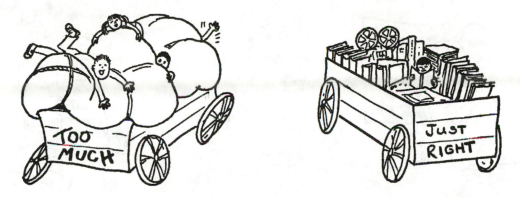

Make the career of the media specialist/librarian an enjoyable one. There are a variety of exciting tasks and many opportunities for creative expression and resourcefulness. In addition, you have the great pleasure of selecting books and other materials as well as the joy of promoting books and reading to children, the satisfaction of working with students of various ages, and the challenge of interacting with all the staff. But like any job, it can become stressful and frustrating. The following are some suggestions that may help you avoid burn-out.

- Have a written, clearly defined job description to build a feeling of security.
- Establish a good relationship with the staff and administration.
- Build a good rapport with the students.
- Prepare a well-planned program of library activities.
- Delegate tasks to assistants and volunteers.
- Attend stimulating, inspirational workshops and seminars.
- Visit other successful library/media centers.
- Allot time to connect with other librarians.
- Arrange book-shopping trips with other librarians.
- Save time for yourself and your family.

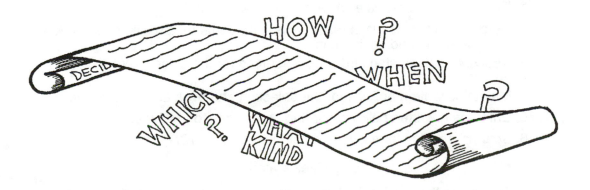

JOB DESCRIPTION FOR SECURITY

Having a written and clearly defined job description for your media center role will give you a feeling of security and confidence as you go about your tasks. Both you and your administrator should have a copy of this job description in your files. Here is a sample job description outlining the various LMC responsibilities. Change or add to it to fit your own particular situation.

Job Description: Library/Instructional Media Specialist

Administrative Duties

1. Develops the LMC programs, its routines, and procedures.
2. Tracks all LMC records.
3. Determines system to be used for checkout of materials.
4. Schedules student and classroom use of the LMC.
5. Establishes behavioral standards for students in the LMC.
6. Supervises both volunteer and paid library assistants.
7. Allocates the use of audiovisual equipment and materials.
8. Coordinates and cooperates with the public and other school libraries.
9. Works with the administration on the budget and goals for the LMC.
10. Promotes the LMC and its programs.

Selection of Materials and Equipment

1. Evaluates and selects all materials and equipment.
2. Determines the needs of teachers and students as a basis for selection of new materials and equipment.
3. Knows and uses standard review sources for the selection of materials and equipment.
4. Maintains written policies for the selection and evaluation of materials.
5. Enforces a written policy regarding challenges to LMC materials.
6. Sets up a policy for acceptance of gifts to the LMC.

Organizes Materials

1. Organizes the LMC collection according to accepted procedures in order that students and teachers can easily locate materials.

2. Processes materials simply and efficiently.

3. Maintains the card catalog — whether manual or computerized.

4. Prepares a periodic inventory of the library's collection.

5. Supervises the withdrawal of worn or out-of-date materials.

Services to Students

1. Establishes an attractive and easily accessible LMC for student use.

2. Guides students in finding and using a wide variety of materials.

3. Informs students of the materials and services available from the LMC through orientation, bulletin boards, handbooks, and class talks.

4. Guides students in developing discrimination in listening and viewing.

5. Helps students become comfortable with new technology.

6. Develops a research and library skills program relating to the needs of the students.

7. Coordinates the LMC activities and materials to student activities in the school.

8. Teaches or provides materials for a class of gifted readers.

9. Helps students find books and materials to satisfy their many curiosities.

10. Attempts to instill in students the ability to be self-learners by promoting the spirit of inquiry and teaching effective fact-finding skills.

11. Promotes reading through reading clubs, storytimes, book talks and bulletin boards.

12. Provides stimulating library activities to interest students in books and reading.

13. Arranges author, illustrator, or storyteller visits for students' enjoyment.

14. Recruits, trains, and supervises student assistants in the LMC.

Services to Teachers

1. Works with teachers in scheduling classes, small groups, and individual students in the LMC.

2. Keeps teachers informed of media services and materials through periodic newsletters.

3. Helps individual teachers by providing all types of materials for their use in their various units of study and for their personal use.

4. Recommends books that teachers can use for classroom read-alouds.

5. Prepares bibliographies on various subjects when needed.

6. Assists teachers in evaluating textbook reading lists.

7. Plans with teachers for meaningful and effective reference work for their students.

8. Holds orientation sessions for new staff members.

9. Serves on schoolwide curriculum committees.

10. Cooperates with any schoolwide programs of instruction.

Once your job description is clearly defined, you can relax knowing that you are fulfilling your responsibilities!

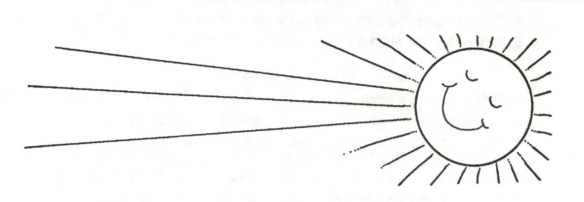

GOOD RELATIONSHIPS WITH STAFF AND ADMINISTRATION

Feeling comfortable with the staff and the administrator promotes a stress-free workplace. Always try to be pleasant and helpful. "Going the extra mile" in finding the right book or audiovisual item for a teacher's use will go far toward building a good relationship. For example:

- Meet frequently with teachers to listen to their needs and problems and to discuss services available to them through you and the LMC.

- Keep a mental or a written list of specific interests of individual teachers so that you can watch for books, magazine articles, and other materials that might be of interest and help to them.

- Set up a file of community resources that might benefit teachers in their instructional units.

- Attend all school programs and meetings.

- Hold short in-service sessions for instruction on new audiovisual equipment.

- Work with teachers and administrators to establish a professional library in the LMC to show your interest in them and their concerns.

For more specific ways to establish good relationships with staff and administrators, see Chapter 6.

Working to establish good relations with all the staff enables you to be happy about your work and eager to come to school each day.

GOOD RAPPORT WITH STUDENTS

Your feelings toward your students and their feelings toward you are of paramount importance in the establishment of an exciting and welcoming LMC. They are also of primary importance in your overall enjoyment of your job.

Your enthusiasm toward the library and its materials will be transferred to the students, and your cheerful greetings and helpful manner will make them feel welcome in the LMC. Make an effort to know the students' needs, abilities, and interests so that you can provide books and other materials for them to use and enjoy. Students feel more a part of the LMC and its programs if they are allowed to have some input in the LMC activities. The following form may be of use. Let students fill it out and hand it in to you. Be sure you let them know the results of the survey, and then act upon it as you plan your programs.

LET'S HEAR YOUR IDEAS!

Help us plan activities for the LMC!

Check the activity that you would like to see offered in the LMC.

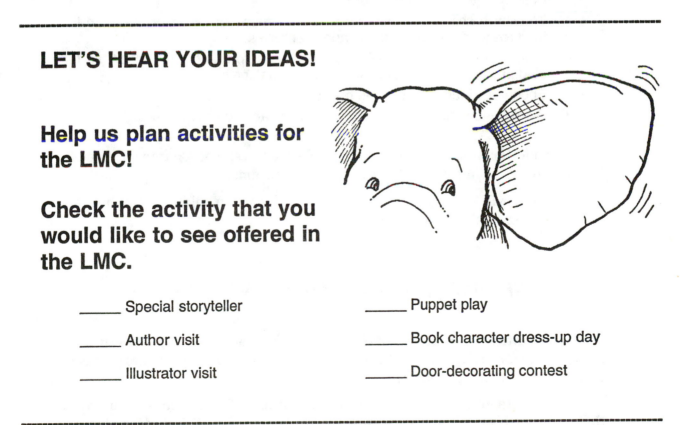

_____ Special storyteller   _____ Puppet play

_____ Author visit   _____ Book character dress-up day

_____ Illustrator visit   _____ Door-decorating contest

There are many ways to build a good rapport between you and your students. Here are just a few suggestions:

- Use your camera to take snapshots of students and their school activities.

- Keep a scrapbook of these snapshots and make it available for students to look at in their free time.
- Encourage creative writing by reading students' poetry or short stories over the intercom once a week.
- Work with children to produce a special in-school television program that features students involved in various activities.
- Keep the LMC open for 20 to 30 minutes before and after school so that students can check out books and other materials.
- Encourage student-produced bulletin boards.
- Display students' artwork, creative writing, and science projects.

For additional ideas on promoting student interest, see Chapter 3, Reading Promotions and Chapter 4, Running Special Programs.

Burnout will never be a problem for you if you can relate to children and share their enthusiasms and interests.

WELL-PLANNED PROGRAM OF LIBRARY ACTIVITIES

The possibilities for exciting LMC programs are endless. Implementing the many program activities will keep you enthusiastic about your work and always on the lookout for new ideas.

A good starting point for implementing these LMC programs is to have a theme for each month and plan your activities around it. Some ideas that you can use for monthly themes are seasons, holidays, friendship, pets, wild animals,

Mother Goose, Native Americans, beach adventures, grandparents, circus, foods, family, kites, movies, fairy tales, science fiction, historical fiction, weather, rocks, solar system, stars and the universe, dinosaurs and other prehistoric animals, travel, book friends, drama, poetry, flags, mythology, knowing your school/state/city/country, transportation, magic, and superstitions.

Once you have chosen your theme, you can incorporate many interest-arousing activities around it. Your bulletin boards, book talks, storytimes, library skills, and monthly contests can all be related to the monthly theme. You can also have special speakers, exhibits, videos, and presentations to enhance the theme. Teachers should be kept informed of the theme because they may want to make use of the theme in their planning. Planning your activities around a theme is very workable — students will enjoy learning about the various subjects, and you will have the satisfaction of having organized a meaningful experience for all.

Once you have experienced the planning and implementation of successful, exciting programs in your LMC, you will be filled with enthusiasm to develop new activities to make your LMC a vibrant center of learning.

See Chapters 3 and 4 for other ideas on running special programs.

An enthusiastic media specialist is never burned out!

DELEGATE TASKS TO ASSISTANTS AND VOLUNTEERS

Even though you may feel that you can do all of the LMC jobs better than anyone else, you will maintain a more comprehensive, efficient, productive, and attractive media center if you are willing to delegate some responsibilities to your assistants, either paid or volunteer.

Decide which responsibilities you wish to reserve for yourself. These will probably include all planning, teaching of classes, selection of materials, choosing materials for teachers' use in their units of study, and budgeting. After you have listed the tasks you plan to do yourself, then list the jobs that can be done by your paid assistant, your adult volunteers, and your student helpers. Find out the various strengths of your assistants so you can delegate tasks for which they are most qualified. To help you ascertain these strengths, use the following survey with your volunteers.

To help us know your skills and interests, please indicate below the tasks that you would most enjoy doing in our LMC.

Typing: _____   Shelving: _____
Book repair: _____   Picture file: _____
Vertical file: _____   Bulletin boards: _____
Filing cards: _____   Working at desk: _____
Helping students: _____ Technology assistant: _____

Name: _____

To help us know your skills and interests, please indicate below the tasks that you would most enjoy doing in our LMC.

Typing: _____   Shelving: _____
Book repair: _____   Picture file: _____
Vertical file: _____   Bulletin boards: _____
Filing cards: _____   Working at desk: _____
Helping students: _____ Technology assistant: _____

Name: _____

(Volunteer Survey)

LMC RESPONSIBILITIES CHART

LMC Specialist

Paid Assistant

Adult Volunteers

Student Volunteers

Remember: Work delegated to others will save you time for the tasks that only you can do!

(Use This Chart to List the Various LMC Duties and Who Will Be Responsible for Them)

ATTEND STIMULATING, INSPIRATIONAL WORKSHOPS AND SEMINARS

From time to time, exciting media workshops will be offered in your area. Try to attend at least one a year. The expense is well worth it, so plan to set aside some funds for this purpose.

You can find professional workshops and seminars on many subjects, including storytelling, new books, author/illustrator presentations, technology, bookmaking, library skills, and program planning. Your local educational media association will also hold yearly (or more frequent) conventions offering workshops on many topics. Local colleges or universities may offer interesting graduate classes in your field.

When you come back from an exciting workshop, seminar, or class, you will doubtless be well-supplied with fresh ideas that you plan to try. Don't file away your notes and printed handouts without trying at least one of them within the next week or two. The ideas you have acquired need to be used quickly while your enthusiasm is high.

On the following page is a permission request form for your principal which explains the workshop, class, or seminar you wish to attend. Unless the workshop or class is not during school hours, you will need his/her permission to attend because a substitute needs to be scheduled. If school funds need to be used for this workshop, permission needs to be granted in any case.

Workshops, seminars, and classes can renew your excitement about your work and help you to avoid burnout.

VISIT OTHER SUCCESSFUL LIBRARY/MEDIA CENTERS

Although workshops and seminars are very stimulating and can be inspirational, the opportunity to visit other media centers also provides numerous ideas that you will want to try. When visiting other media centers, you can get ideas for room arrangements, bulletin boards, scheduling, library skills, theme ideas, activities, games, and contests. While even experienced media specialists get much from such visits, they are especially helpful to new librarian/media specialists.

If you have not yet computerized your LMC but are planning to do so, it is extremely important to visit media centers that are computerized in order to compare the various computer programs available. Discuss with each media specialist the advantages and disadvantages of their computer system and take careful notes to help you in your choice for your center.

These visits to other LMCs need to be planned during the school day, but they can sometimes be arranged during times when you have no scheduled classes. This means that you will not need a substitute.

Perhaps after visiting several media centers you will feel that your own center has much to offer in the way of creative ideas. Inviting other media specialists to visit your LMC will inspire you to be even more creative and productive.

Following are forms both for visiting other media centers and for inviting other specialists to your LMC. Get out and about and learn something new!

PERMISSION REQUEST FORM

Date: _____

I request permission to attend the following: workshop _____

    seminar _____

    class _____

    convention _____

It will be held at _____ on _____
                    (Place)   *(Date)*

My attendance at this event will help me in my work in the LMC in the following ways:

_____

_____

_____

_____

Substitute required: yes _____ no _____   Cost to the district: _____

I request that the funds for this activity be taken from _____
                                                      (Funding Category)

Thank You.

_____, Librarian

(Permission Form for Workshops and Seminars — print on school letterhead and
then attach brochure or advertisement describing the workshop)

Date: _____

Permission is requested to visit the _____ Media Center on

_____ from _____ to _____.
          (Date)   (Time)   (Time)

I would like to visit this center in order to observe: _____

_____

_____

Thank you.

_____, Librarian

                    _____ Media Center

PLEASE COME!

Date: _____

Dear _____:

I would like to invite you to our media center

on _____

at _____ o'clock.

You may be interested in seeing our _____

_____

_____

We hope you will join us at this time.

Sincerely,

_____, Media Specialist

(Forms for Requesting Permission to Visit Another LMC and for Inviting Media Specialists to Visit your LMC)

TIME TO CONNECT WITH OTHER LIBRARIANS

There is nothing more helpful to librarian/media specialists than to get together. "Talking shop" with others in the field is worthwhile in many ways. The ideas that you obtain from such an interchange can be very valuable. Many times you may have a problem that another media specialist has encountered and solved. His/her experience and those of the others may give you a totally different outlook on the problem and how to solve it. At times, a new book or periodical may be shared which will help you in the process of selecting new materials. Other times someone may have a new game or library skill activity that can be used by the others. Discussions on computerized systems, use of assistants and volunteers, author visits, storyteller presentations, scheduling, and special programs are all helpful. Sometimes a media center newsletter can be shared with the others.

You will also find that this time together provides a good opportunity to share materials as well as ideas. For instance, you may have inadvertently bought duplicate copies of a certain title and then realized that you do not need both. Trading these duplicate copies with another media specialist who also has unwanted titles is often a happy solution for both of you. Sometimes additional copies of a certain title are temporarily needed by you or a member of your staff. The other media specialists may be able to lend you the necessary copies. Occasionally, even pieces of equipment are shared by various media centers.

If possible, plan a regular weekly meeting with media specialists in your district to exchange ideas and materials. A weekly lunch-time meeting works well since after-school time is often filled with other meetings and obligations.

Connect with your colleagues to avoid burnout.

BOOK-SHOPPING TRIPS WITH OTHER LIBRARIANS

For a very productive book selection trip, plan your book shopping with other librarian/media specialists. As you shop, other librarians will point out books that they feel to be excellent choices. They will undoubtedly be familiar with some books which you are not and vice versa. Occasionally, in the case of a very expensive book, you and another librarian may arrange to share the cost and the book.

As you browse through the aisles, you will exchange many ideas on which books can be used for storytelling, book talks, special units, slow readers, and gifted readers. You will also get ideas on the best choices for books in a content area and ideas on how to use them.

Often district media specialists will plan these book-buying trips for an entire day so that they can visit several book suppliers. You will naturally have lunch together, where more ideas can be exchanged. You can learn much from one another and become better acquainted.

These trips need not disrupt your regular LMC schedule, which would upset the teachers, students, and staff. They can be scheduled for the very beginning of the school year before your regular schedule has begun, or they can be planned for conference or in-service days. If your administrator realizes the benefits to be gained from these buying trips together, he/she will certainly be in favor of it.

Avoid book-buying burnout by arranging book-shopping trips with other librarians!

SAVE TIME FOR YOURSELF AND YOUR FAMILY

Even though your life seems to be centered around your LMC, complete absorption in your job may cause that "burned-out" feeling. It is important that you have a life outside your media center. Maintain your old interests and even develop new ones from time to time.

Exercise and regular good eating habits ensure your general good health and enable you to do your best in your home and at school. Save time before or after school for a brisk walk with a fellow staff member or a family member.

Your mental health is as important as your physical health. The previous pages have suggested ways in which you can be successful in your work, but you also need to feel successful in your family and home life, too.

Guard your evenings and weekends. Try not to spend long hours after school. Learn to prioritize, and realize that you will never get everything done. Don't feel guilty if everything you planned to do is not accomplished. Your well-organized LMC and library program will enable you to close your doors at a reasonable hour and go home to spend quality time with your family and friends.

Balance your home and school life to avoid burnout!